Praise for

Look at It This Way

"No one gets to the point like Jan Silvious. Compelling and eye opening, the message of *Look at It This Way* is truly life changing. Its spiritual truths are immediately applicable and practical. Full of light-bulb moments."

—BABBIE MASON, Dove Award–winning singer and songwriter; speaker and author

"Jan Silvious is witty, wonderful, and wise. This book is pure Jan. You will laugh out loud, stop and think, and gratefully pick up the gems of wisdom lovingly wrapped in each page for you."

—SHEILA WALSH, Women of Faith speaker and author of *All That Really Matters*

"Very few people express biblical truths in real-life terms as well as Jan Silvious. She truly allows us to understand the wisdom of the Word of God and teaches us how to apply it to our daily lives. Jan's writing offers not just nuggets of truth, but a whole treasure chest of jewels!"

—KATHY TROCCOLI, author, speaker, and recording artist

"I love books with practical, sensible information, and *Look at It This Way* by my friend Jan Silvious is one of those. Every page is a powerhouse of truth for our lives."

—LUCI SWINDOLL, author and Women of Faith speaker

"With 20/20 vision of the issues women face, Jan uses these pages to open our eyes to the problem, process, and progress of hitting our issues head on. With painstaking passion, she pens the principles that can produce the power that can help us live through the eyes of possibilities."

—THELMA WELLS, author, Women of Faith speaker,
and professor at Master's Divinity School and Graduate
School of Divinity

"Being Jan's friend is like holding the mirror of God's Word to your face and seeing yourself as you are. She is direct, astute, and wise. As you enter these pages, you will feel embraced, understood, and equipped to face life head on."

—PATSY CLAIRMONT, Women of Faith speaker
and author of *Mending Your Heart in a Broken World*

"Jan Silvious is a positive thinking, upbeat, no-nonsense writer who could change the world!"

—MARILYN MEBERG, author of *The Zippered Heart* and
Women of Faith speaker

"Jan Silvious is that one person I trust to look me straight in the face and say, 'Your grid is bent, and this is how you can fix it.' Her loving honesty, wisdom, wit, and perspectives on life are a practical guide to help us live with purpose, power, and productivity."

—ALICIA WILLIAMSON, author of *Hold Nothing Back*

"Jan has a way of getting to the bottom line. She is like a searchlight moving over the dark waters looking for a response to the all-encompassing questions she loves to ask: 'Where is it written? Where is the truth? Where is the lie?'"

—KAY ARTHUR, cofounder of Precept Ministries
International

LOOK
AT IT
THIS
W A Y

LOOK AT IT THIS WAY

Straightforward Wisdom
to Put Life in Perspective

JAN SILVIOUS

WATERBROOK
PRESS

LOOK AT IT THIS WAY
PUBLISHED BY WATERBROOK PRESS
12265 Oracle Boulevard, Suite 200
Colorado Springs, Colorado 80921
A division of Random House Inc.

ISBN 978-0-30744-492-9

The Library of Congress cataloged the hardcover edition as follows:
Silvious, Jan, 1944–
    Look at it this way : straightforward wisdom to put life in perspective /
Jan Silvious.—1st ed.
        p. cm.
    ISBN 1-57856-693-2
    1. Christian life. I. Title.
BV4501.3 .S58 2003
248.4—dc21   2002151342

Printed in the United States of America
2008—First Trade Paperback Edition

10 9 8 7 6 5 4 3 2 1

To my mother,
who told me a long time ago to "look at it this way!"
Thank you for your wisdom!
I will forever be grateful that I had a mother like you.

CONTENTS

LOOK AT IT THIS WAY

Your view of life determines how you live life. It is not your circumstances. It is not what someone has said to you or how someone has treated you or the breaks that have or have not come your way. It's all about how you *see* those events and encounters. It's all about your thoughts, your perceptions—the grid through which you view life.

How do you view the things that have happened to you?

How have you interpreted them?

Each of us has a grid through which we look at our world. Yours has been formed by your childhood experiences, the people you know, your own emotional makeup, and the various events that happen in your world. Your grid significantly affects how well you are going to live.

For you see, in many ways we can be like a group of dogs that were put through an experiment in the 1960s. They were placed in raised cages that were divided into sides that had a doggie-size hole between them. At the beginning of the experiment, the researchers sent a mild electric shock to one side of the cage. Naturally, the dogs went to the other side, which felt safe and comfortable. But then things changed. The researchers sent electric shocks to both sides of the cage. For a little while, the dogs went back and forth between the two sides, but when it became clear that no matter where they landed, they would be shocked, the dogs simply stopped trying. Even after the current was turned off on one side of the cage, and the dogs could easily walk away from their discomfort, most stayed put and never again tried to find a way to avoid the shock. Their past experiences had taught them that they could not escape from the shock—or so they thought—and because they *thought* it was impossible, for them it was. Only a few ever attempted to check out the other side of the cage.

This experiment was modified later for two-legged animals like you and me, and the results showed that certain people had an "impossibility" mind-set. They believed they had no control over the things that happened to them and that they could not change the way things were. In other words, any problems they were facing would be ongoing, pervasive, and totally inescapable. Sadly, for most of them that kind of thinking became self-fulfilling.[1]

People with an impossibility mind-set have a grid that is bent. They see problems and think there are no solutions for them. They can even see problems where there are none. But if their grids can be straightened so that they can see possibilities and answers for the tough places in life, they have unlimited potential for moving on.

If your grid is bent, I have good news for you. A warped grid can be made straight, and *Look at It This Way* is meant to be a grid-straightening adventure. I invite you to join me as we tackle the great, exhilarating challenge of embracing a healthy view of life and all its glorious possibilities. A straight grid will enable you to experience blessings you have never imagined.

Presented in the following chapters are ten maxims for having a grid that is healthy and well managed. These principles may be a major shift in thinking for you. You may find yourself bumping up against long-held perceptions, resulting in a certain amount of emotional and even spiritual distress. But I assure you, if you will embrace these axioms and put them into practice, no matter what is going on or how you feel, you will be a changed person. As your grid-straightening skills increase, so will your emotional well-being and your spiritual confidence. In turn, you will experience ever-improving relationships and greater peace.

Here's to your grid and here's to your life!

THIS IS ONE EVENT IN A LIFETIME OF EVENTS

We should be careful to get out of an experience only the wisdom that is in it—and stop there; lest we be like the cat that sits down on a hot stove-lid. She will never sit down on a hot stove-lid again—and that is well; but also she will never sit down on a cold one anymore.

—MARK TWAIN

I can remember sitting in a car, mulling over the news I'd just been told. "We've decided to give the book project to someone else." I couldn't believe my ears. A friend who was also a colleague had asked me to write a book for our organization, and I'd spent a lot of time and energy trying to do what she had asked. I was trusting, somewhat inexperienced, and clearly naive. I had thought that since she had given me this assignment, I would be allowed to see it through. I believe in finishing what I start. But rather than allowing me to revise the manuscript until I got it right, she had cavalierly taken me off the project. Another better-known writer was called in, and that was that. End of discussion.

I kept telling myself that I had done nothing to deserve this dismissal. I could write, and I had worked hard and was willing to do whatever else might be needed. Why hadn't I been given that chance? What was I unable to produce that someone else could? I wanted to vent my anger and frustration. I wanted to have my say, but this decision was out of my control, and for the life of me, it seemed so wrong. What did it say about my competence, value, and giftedness? What did this say about my relationship to this colleague and the level of trust that I had assumed existed between us? I felt hurt, confused, and unsettled.

In the months following, I knew I had to make a choice. Either I could give up writing, consider myself a loser, and nurse this wound for all it was worth, or I could look at this disappointment for what it was—simply one event in a lifetime of events—and go on. And go on I did.

In retrospect, the loss of that book project truly was just one event in my life. It wasn't the end of my writing career, nor was it a statement of my value and competence. But when it happened, it felt like it was. When it happened, it felt highly significant. When it happened, it seemed life defining. But today, fifteen years later, this painful experience seems inconsequential, simply a memory of a difficult time in my life.

WE GET TO CHOOSE

I first heard the words, "This is one event in a lifetime of events. We must move on," several years ago while I was watching a news report about a young woman who went into a schoolyard and shot several children. This was before this kind of tragedy had become a familiar event. The news media was on the scene, prowling from person to person, asking questions, waiting for some distraught individual to declare some experiential finality to the episode.

The news reports kept interrupting the programming that day, and as I watched, the deliberate words and calm demeanor of one particular teacher at the school impressed me. Obviously a seasoned veteran, she kept her expression serene. As the reporter jammed the microphone in her face, this teacher spoke in measured words. "This is one event in a lifetime of events. We must go on."

How could she say that with such conviction in light of the mayhem that had just occurred?

Hadn't children been killed?

Hadn't little bodies been wounded?

Hadn't parents' hopes and dreams been shattered?

Hadn't the assumed security of an elementary school been breached?

Hadn't teachers and students been traumatized?

Hadn't it been a horrible event?

Hadn't people's lives been changed forever?

Yes, yes, yes to every question. No denying the event was tragic and horrible. No denying those people's lives had been forever altered. Grief had invaded their worlds. No doubt they would never be the same, *but* was this to be THE DEFINING EVENT of their lives? Were they to live the rest of their days as victims of a deranged woman with no sense of right and wrong? Would her insane actions fill and control their thoughts for as long as they lived? Would their losses define the quality of their lives? Or could they have a perspective that would restore their balance?

According to this wise teacher, they could. She understood that, as tragic as this event was, it didn't have to define their lives from that day forward. Her words penetrated my heart and resonated as truth. I sensed I had heard something profound and true that I needed to embrace.

Life is a series of events in a lifetime of events, a series of seasons in a lifetime of seasons. How you look at what happens to you will determine your success, your peace, and your sense of well-being and will ultimately tell the tale of a life well lived or a life badly wasted. Harmful events may come your way: illness, divorce, abandonment, molestation, betrayal, or loss, to name a few. You can choose to examine these grid-bending experiences and make the courageous choice to hold on to the truth that "This is one event in a lifetime of events. I will go on. I will not allow any circumstance or opinion to determine who I am, what I think about myself, and how I present myself to other people."

Your viewpoint doesn't have to be molded by concrete perceptions that won't budge. You can choose to control the way your mind interprets events and experiences. Others may have opinions and tell you what they think, but the final interpretation always lies with you. But if you let one event or season of life define all of your life as hard, difficult, and limited, you will have a bent grid that limits you to a one-dimensional view of yourself and your life. If you allow a negative event or comment to define who you are, then you have allowed it to control you.

This truth holds in our victories as well as our defeats. Success, prosperity, good fortune, good times, and good friends may come to us, as well as failure, poverty, tough times, lousy days, and disappointing friends. In some sort of hard-to-see drama, it's all part of a big plan for us.

No matter what, even when the event is very good, we have to move on. The football hero can't stay the hero. Eventually, he has to take off his jersey and face the reality of being an average Joe in the working world. Those touchdowns, long remembered and often rehearsed, comprise only one small part of a lifetime of events. If he wants to live, he has to go on. And so do we.

If we don't, we might end up like King Saul. We read his story in the Bible in the book of First Samuel.

WHEN WE STAY STUCK

King Saul, the first monarch of ancient Israel, just could not get past the threat of losing his throne and his popularity to a handsome young man named David. David's successes eventually overwhelmed everything in the old king's life.

It wasn't always that way. When David killed the great menace of Israel, the Philistine giant, Goliath, it was a love fest between the two men. The aging monarch was thrilled.

> Whatever Saul asked David to do, David did it successfully. So Saul made him a commander in his army, an appointment that was applauded by the fighting men and officers alike. (1 Samuel 18:5)

But when the army was returning home after David had killed Goliath, the king began to hear the sound of tambourines and cymbals. There was rejoicing in the streets of Israel, but it had nothing to do with him. As he and his men made their way to his palace, they encountered a scene that Saul couldn't erase from his mind. Women were dancing in the streets with incredible joy, singing, "Saul has killed his thousands, and David his ten thousands" (verse 7). Jealousy rose up in Saul's heart and consumed him. His rage overwhelmed him, and all that he might have been was destroyed in his jealousy over David's success.

Nothing could quiet his soul. He could not and would not move on. He saw it as wrong, despicable, and terrible that David was the people's favorite. It ought not be, and he, the one and only king, refused to accept it. His interpretation of David's popularity had him caught in a trap from which he couldn't release himself. Sadly, Saul never moved on. He couldn't get rid of David. He sensed he had already lost his throne, and he couldn't regain it. But "David continued to succeed in everything he did, for the LORD was with him. When Saul recognized this, he became even more afraid of him. But all Israel and Judah loved David because he was so successful at leading his troops into battle" (1 Samuel 18:14-16).

As he grew old, Saul's bitterness over David's popularity defined him. We remember him as a weak, angry, ineffective king. His grid was rusty, bent, and unyielding. His legacy was bitterness, jealousy, and tragedy. Saul died never having gotten past David's success and popularity.

Anytime you allow ONE event or season of life to define you, your life, for all intents and purposes, is over. It stops at that event. Even though you continue to breathe, you are not really living. You have stopped growing and learning. You are in gridlock. Recognizing that, you are faced with a choice. Will you remain stuck, or will you decide to pursue mental and emotional health? You have the power to look at a situation, evaluate it for what it is, and then choose what to do with it. This gives *you* the power over the effect of the event.

I will never forget a woman I met years ago who had allowed one event to define her. A pastor's widow, she spent her days sitting in her dead husband's study, listening to tapes of his sermons. She could not come to grips with his death. Her role as a pastor's wife had defined her personhood, and when her husband died, so did she in a thousand ways. Oh, she continued to breathe, but she felt her life no longer had purpose. In her mind, when her role came to a close, so did her life. She did not see how she could go on.

Nor will I forget the man who always introduced himself as the youngest CEO of a particular company. Never mind that he was in his sixties and had long since lost his grip and glamour as the youngest hotshot CEO in his corporate world. He had not grown and moved on as his position and role in the company changed. Sadly, no one seemed to care about this man's "accomplishment" but him.

THERE'S ANOTHER WAY TO LOOK AT LIFE

I, too, have had my moment in the spotlight. When I was a teenager, I was crowned Queen Crester at Camp Crestridge for Girls in Ridgecrest, North Carolina. In that time and place, I truly was a queen. It was an honor every camper longed for. When I go back to visit that camp these days, forty years later, how easy it is to slip into being Queen Crester again—reliving my "glory days"! But what would have happened if I had stayed there, never progressing beyond being the queen in a group of 180 campers? Nothing worse than ending up as an old queen who has no kingdom!

But my coronation was simply *one event* in a lifetime of events.

Eventually, the queen has to put up her crown, the cheerleader has to put up her pompoms, and we have to take our place with other mortal women at the supermarket, squeezing the same fruits and vegetables for their freshness. Our days of adulation and adoration are long gone. We have to choose to go on.

One of my heroes is a wonderful therapist who has taught me invaluable truths. Early in her marriage her husband had abandoned her and their two young children. She was a dependent soul who did not know how to set her watch or drive a car. She realized one day that retreating from life and living in a world of depression was not doing her or her children any good. She was a woman of faith who remembered these words from the Bible: "The LORD appeared... from afar, saying, 'I have loved you with an everlasting love; therefore I have drawn you with lovingkindness'" (Jeremiah 31:3, NASB).

This was an epiphany for her. She got up, got herself together, and began to move on. She pursued life with a passion. She and her girls began the adventure of their lifetimes. She became a psychotherapist, earned her Ph.D., and authored an incredible number of life-changing books.

Her husband's abandonment forever altered her life and world. She could have continued to see herself as a victim, but she made a choice, the choice to move on. That freed her—and her daughters—to live the life they were intended to live!

When you are ready to move on, you have to look at what has you held you back and then blast it with the truth. You may feel timid about that at first. You may be saying, "But if I move on, then I am not acknowledging how bad or how good the past was." Or you may be afraid to let go of something good because you are afraid you will never again receive glory and recognition. You may be afraid to let go of something bad because you think there may be something you can do to "fix it" that you haven't yet discovered. You may be fearful of letting go of someone's actions toward you because you think you must hold that person accountable.

But here's the deal. After you have acknowledged that the event (good or bad) that holds you was simply one event in a lifetime of events, you can choose to move on. This perspective makes life an enjoyable adventure. Every day is different, some days full of joy and laughter, others full of sorrow and pain, but all are part of the "big picture" God intends for us. Wisdom teaches us that no one event or season defines an entire life. Oh, there may be heroic moments that will be remembered, but even heroes live their lives over a lifetime, not just for that moment of grand courage.

During this incredibly surreal season of war we are experiencing in the United States, Todd Beamer has emerged as a hero. He was a young Christian father seated on American Airlines Flight 93, the plane that crashed in Pennsylvania. As the story has been pieced together, it seems Todd recognized that his plane was being hijacked, and he called an operator to tell her what was happening. Through this operator, Todd and his fellow passengers became aware that two planes had been flown into the World Trade Center towers. Realizing that what was happening on his plane was somehow related to those horrendous attacks and that he was probably going to die, Todd and some of the other passengers decided on a plan of action. With great resolution, Todd asked the operator to say the Lord's Prayer with him.

He told her he wanted to be sure he was clear with Jesus. Then, having put things in order, Todd said those now famous words: "Let's roll."

With several other passengers, Todd rushed the cockpit. According to the flight recorder recovered from the crash, a ferocious fight ensued as the passengers moved in to prevent the plane from reaching its deadly destination—possibly the Capitol of the United States. Everyone on board died in a fiery crash in a barren field in Pennsylvania. Todd Beamer and his fellow passengers who stood to say, "No, you won't take us down without a fight," will always be remembered for this event. Mission on earth accomplished.

For Todd and his fellow passengers, this tragic event was the final event in a lifetime of events. But according to his wife, Lisa, Todd's life was made up of many wonderful, powerful events. She has memory upon memory of special times and the great character with which Todd lived his life.

However, September 11, 2001, is also one event in a lifetime of events for Lisa Beamer. She has been an amazing example of stability in the midst of great tragedy. Whenever you see her on television, she is serene and stable, even though she is obviously in sorrow. I caught an interview where she said, "I am trying to focus on what I still have, not on what I have lost." This young widow and mother knows that no matter what happens, we must go on.

America as a nation also must go on. September 11, 2001, is one event in our national lifetime of events. It was tragic and horrifying, and it caused us to shake our heads in disbelief as we were attacked and victimized on our own soil for the first time in our history. But go on we must. If we fail to do so, we will allow those who hate us and desire our destruction to win.

The emotions that follow painful events—shame, blame, depression, anger, grief, and denial—will define our lives unless we choose the perspective that every event in life, even a tragic one, is merely one event in a lifetime of events. The pain is real, the impact is certain, but if you allow yourself to be defined forever by what is said or not said, by what is done or not done, by what is given or taken, you give those events, circumstances, and words greater power than they ever deserve.

If we are to free ourselves from the pain of these events, we must work through our emotions; we must face them and release them so they don't remain bottled inside our hearts, distorting our perspective. And the decision must ultimately be made—"Let's roll!"

IT'S UP TO YOU

What about you? Do you have a moment that keeps defining you? Do you go back to "that moment" and see yourself as frozen in time? Do you feel good about yourself when you are recognized for being the football hero, the youngest CEO, or even "the queen"? Do you require the affirming words of those around you to feel that you are worthwhile? Have you latched on to a comment and made it your mantra for whether you will even try again to succeed in an area where you may have failed?

Perhaps you are thinking about an event that has been at the forefront of your mind for years. Maybe it is something that happened that you can't get out of your mind. Maybe it's a memory of something said that you want to forget but haven't. Well, one thing's for sure. You won't "just forget." You can't change history or wipe out memory or pretend something really significant didn't happen. That is called denial.

Denial is never an answer for anything. It is like sweeping the floor, looking around for a dustpan and sweeping the dirt under the rug. It is failure to face the facts. You can't move forward until you recognize what happened for what it was. You can't pretend it wasn't so bad or that it wasn't so wonderful. Grief has to be felt. Anger must be acknowledged. Depression has to be confronted with hope.

So what do you do?

The healthiest move you can make is to *look at the event for what it was.*

Examine it.

Handle it.

Acknowledge how it made you feel.

Look at the damage it caused.

Look at the high you experienced.

Look at the person you were when it happened.

Admit how you have responded to the event since it happened.

Ask yourself if you are pleased with how the event affected you.

Once you have taken stock of "the event," you are ready to make the deliberate move away from it so that you can move on. Ask yourself, "What is the worst thing that can happen if I move on?" Do you think:

- *I will be rejected.*
- *I'll make a fool of myself and be embarrassed.*
- *I will fail.*
- *I will be going into unknown territory. I will be afraid.*
- *People will be angry with me for changing.*

This exercise is a great way to begin to move forward. When you come up with the answer, it may scare you to death…but wait a minute. How catastrophic is it, really? When you look at these scary thoughts through a straight grid, you begin to see that they are not catastrophic. They may be painful, but they are not the end of the world. I have felt similar things before, and you know what? They didn't kill me. I didn't enjoy the experiences, but I am still alive!

About the time I was reigning as Queen Crester and enjoying my success, I had to give a little speech and quote some scripture. When I stood to give my speech, I froze. Everyone else, of course, remembered their parts. I was disappointed in myself, but I held it together until one of the leaders of the group said, "Too bad you forgot all that scripture!" Well, at that point I became a teenage basket case. Not only did I forget the scripture, but now I was sobbing in front of everyone.

I probably held on to that event longer than I should have. For years I resisted public speaking because I was afraid I would forget what I was supposed to say. I was afraid of that panicky feeling akin to standing in the middle of the freeway during rush hour. Eventually though, I had to get past that paralyzing experience and see it as just one event in a lifetime of events. Now, public speaking is *what* I do. I no longer feel panicky or anxious when I walk up on a platform.

Are you holding on to events that were too painful or to things that people have done to you that have left you bleeding? Do you see yourself as a certain kind of person because of something unfortunate that has happened in your life?

If so, today might be a good day to put that event behind you and, with God's help, go on. Don't allow yourself to continue to be identified by the past. If you want to move to the next level of maturity and insight, it's time to look at your circumstances differently. Start today by telling yourself: Whatever happens, it is one event in a lifetime of events. I must go on!

And then, my friend, do it!

TWO

WHAT MIGHT HAVE BEEN DOES NOT EXIST

For all the sad words of tongue or pen, the saddest are these: *It might have been.*

—JOHN GREENLEAF WHITTIER

A kitchen counter may seem a small thing in the grand scheme of life, but to a woman, it can be pretty significant. I am that woman, and the kitchen counter is mine. Every morning when I come down for breakfast and every evening when I leave the kitchen after dinner, I see the long, curving albatross that is my kitchen counter. Eight people can sit around it comfortably, and it is bright RED.

I have always wanted a red kitchen counter. So when we had to change the stovetop, which required a new counter, I decided to do something really exciting. I chose to install a very long and very wide red counter. When you walk into my kitchen, you see a RED counter.

Now, I have made peace with my counter. I have made peace with the fact that I chose it. I have made peace with the fact that it will be a long time before I can replace it. I HAVE made peace! But I can tell you it took me awhile! Thoughts of would have, should have, and could have flooded my brain. *Why didn't you think this through better? Why didn't you stick with what you had? Why didn't you consider what that much red would do to a room? Why didn't you ask an interior designer to give an opinion?* Why, why, why?

When these kinds of questions pop into our brains, the best thing we can tell ourselves is, *But you didn't, so why even go there?* We spend so much emotional energy dealing with what might have been instead of what is, we are left exhausted with nothing to show for it. Wisdom says that if change is not an option, let it be.

IT'S A DEAD END

I have met so many people who invest enormous amounts of time looking back at what might have been. Frequently when I speak, I ask, "What are some of your what-might-have-been thoughts?" The answers are universal and usually come out in this order:

What if I had...

> *married someone else?*
>
> *never married?*
>
> *married?*
>
> *had fewer children?*
>
> *had children?*
>
> *gone to college?*
>
> *had a different career?*
>
> *come from a different family?*
>
> *become a Christian sooner?*
>
> *been kinder to some relative who is now dead?*

Whenever I hear these laments, I answer bluntly, "But you didn't so don't even go there!"

Longing for what might have been is one of the most nonproductive, futile ways we can spend our time. Regret never changes what is.

Sometimes we can see this more easily in other people than we can in ourselves, so let me tell you about Angela. Angela married her best friend, or so she thought. Before they married, she and Jack could talk for hours on end. But once they said their vows, it wasn't long before he shut down and they became like strangers. Jack was faithful and pleasant, and he worked hard to provide for them, but he was no longer interested in what Angela had done during the day or in what she thought about. Believing that marriage should be more than coexistence, she asked if they could go for counseling. Jack responded, "For what? I don't have a problem. You can go if you want to, but I am fine with the way things are."

Angela felt trapped and hopeless. She had no godly reason to leave the marriage—nor did she have a reason to want to stay in it. But her grid made her prone to second-guessing, and all she could do was beat herself up for marrying Jack, thinking about what her life might have been if she hadn't married him. Angela always struggled with making decisions, and it seemed that whenever she made one, she lived to regret it. Regret then consumed her so that she couldn't see anything positive or any hope that God would intervene and cause "all things to work together for good" (Romans 8:28, NASB). She lived her life looking in a rearview mirror. She focused on what she had missed and on what might have been if she had done things differently. If only she had known what she knows now!

Angela needs a reality check. All of her regrets would never help her change what had already happened. In fact, they kept her from looking at what she could do to improve her marriage.

Perhaps you have also made a choice that has altered the landscape of your life. If so, my heart goes out to you—but that still doesn't change what is. Like Angela, you need to move on. Your life is your life. It is the material you have been given to work with.

Whatever you are dealing with is what you are dealing with. That includes the good, the bad, and the ugly. Be thankful for the good, and gracefully and patiently endure the bad, knowing that God will use it to make you who he wants you to be. While I don't think we're supposed to welcome the ugly—the perverse, the abusive, the ungodly—we *can* accept it as part of our life and move on. All of your wishes to the contrary won't change what has happened to you. God knows that it is part of your experience, and he won't waste it.

If you focus on what might have been, you are at a dead end. Think about it. Whether you find out that your friend bought an outfit for $69 that you paid $169 for a month earlier, or that a job you passed up is taking off with all kinds of opportunities, if you spend time thinking about what you could have had, you will absolutely end up depressed. In fact, since much depression is "anger turned inward," self-blame for what might have been can lead you down a path of ongoing sadness. *If only* and *I should have* will dot your thinking and permeate your emotions. Both will kill you. They may kill you slowly, but they will kill you. They will kill your will to keep going, your desire to trust God, and your hope that God will actually override your choices by causing them to work together for good.

If you look at another person and think, *I could be happy if I had her life,* then you assume that everything would be the same for you if you had her position, possessions, or relationships. But you are only fooling yourself. You can never live another person's life. You bring in a different element, and you change everything. Sometimes our grids are so bent we fail to realize that our view is limited and that there is a lot we can't see or know. If you haven't been behind another person's closed doors, you have no idea if his or her life is as idyllic as it may seem.

Most of all, if you focus on what might have been, you miss what can be. Dan was fired from a job he thought he loved. In fact, if you asked him, he did love it. The whole firing episode had been unfortunate and unfair. The company was in a financial squeeze, and Dan and two of his coworkers were let go. They weren't really given explanations for their pink slips, except that their department was costing the firm money instead of producing it. Dan knew that wasn't exactly the truth, but what could he do? The company needed to cut some salaries, and he and his coworkers were among the top-salaried workers. Such is life.

For several weeks he and his wife, Sarah, spent most of their time rehashing what could have been. Dan kept asking, "Why didn't I see this coming?" "I should have done something differently." "I really liked this job. How am I ever going to move up in my career and find a job I like?" They took the layoff personally, saying that Dan's boss had never liked Dan and that if he had really been valued, he would not have been laid off. After all he had done for the company, he still ended up being dumped.

Then six weeks from the time he was fired, Dan almost miraculously had a turnaround in his thinking. He woke up one morning and thought, *This is getting me nowhere.* He made his way into the kitchen and said to Sarah, "Tell me if this is true. Yes, I liked the job. Yes, it was a raw deal to be fired. Yes, I really wish it hadn't

happened, but it did, and wishing it hadn't isn't helping us any, is it?"
Sarah nodded.

"I need to move past this, don't I?" Dan asked. Again, his wife
nodded.

Dan had reached a very powerful conclusion: I best get my eyes
off what might have been and begin thinking about what can be. Dan
decided there was no time like the present to begin looking at the
future. He did some serious soul searching about his part in being laid
off and about what he really wanted to do. Dan then took responsibility for his own life and moved on. Two months later he was interview-
ing for a dream job that he never would have even thought about
pursuing had he not let go of what might have been.

We often tend to view what-might-have-been as the place where
the grass is greenest. Maybe it would have been wonderful, maybe
not. You'll never know, so what's the point of keeping that your focus?
Old boyfriends, old girlfriends, old job opportunities, and old offers
for the trip of a lifetime—they all belong in a trash pile labeled: It
Doesn't Exist, So Don't Go There!

EVEN IN LOSS, YOU MUST MOVE ON

This is true, even in grief. Whenever you experience loss, you will be
tempted to think about what might have been—which initially is
healthy and necessary. We need to grieve what might have been in
order to work through the emotions that follow loss. In the initial
aftermath of loss, you have to give yourself (and others) enough time

to let the reality of the loss sink in before you can begin to move forward. Your mind and heart have to process all the possible scenarios and the what-ifs before you will be able to move forward by telling yourself that what might have been does not exist. The greater the magnitude of the loss, the longer the time needed.

But even with loss, the time eventually comes when we must shift our focus from what might have been to what still can be. Mrs. Job, a classic figure in the Scriptures, is a woman who suffered great losses but never moved beyond them. She could see no way to go on, and she certainly was no help to her patient, long-suffering, God-honoring husband.

God and Job had an up-front relationship. God knew what he could expect out of Job, and Job knew what he could expect out of God. They were at home with one another; as at home as you can be when one of you is God and one of you is a mortal.

Job was the richest man in the territory—truth be told, he was likely the richest man in the world. He had more livestock and land than anyone else. Not only was he a man of great wealth, he was a man of outstanding integrity. He was blameless before the Lord. That can't be said for many of us, but Mr. Job had it said of him.

Satan came on the scene and had a word with God about Mr. Job. Now the thing that was interesting was that although Satan started the conversation by stating that he had been out looking around, it was God who asked, "Did you notice my man Job? He is a man of integrity, and he will have nothing to do with evil." God brought Job into the conversation, and Satan, opportunist that he is, decided to jump on this chance to give God a hard time. Satan said, "No wonder Job is so wonderful and has such integrity. You have done nothing but bless him and protect him. Of course, he is going to speak well of you. Who wouldn't?"

God said, "Okay, Satan, you can test Job. You can take away everything he has, but you can't touch his body."

Satan slithered away and made his strike.

Bad news travels quickly, and Mr. Job began to hear the tragic reports almost immediately. An out-of-breath runner claimed, "Your livestock has been stolen; your field hands have been killed." Then another: "Your sheep and shepherds have all burned up in a firestorm." Then another: "Your camels are gone and your camel handlers are all dead." Still reeling with the first three reports of tragedy, Job saw a fourth messenger headed his way. This one brought the worst news of all: "Your children were all having a meal at their brother's house, and a great wind came; the house collapsed and killed them all. Mr. Job, your children are dead."

Can you imagine what must have been going through Job's head? He had just lost everything he owned and just about everything he cared about, left with next to nothing. Here's what happened next:

[When the word came about his children,] Job stood up and tore his robe in grief. Then he shaved his head and fell to the ground before God. He said,

"I came naked from my mother's womb,
    and I will be stripped of everything when I die.

The LORD gave me everything I had,
and the LORD has taken it away.
Praise the name of the LORD!"

In all of this, Job did not sin by blaming God. (Job 1:20-22)

I find Job quite amazing. The news that hit him was devastating, but he was not devastated. He seems to have had a perfectly straight grid when it came to his view of God and his dealings with humanity. But Satan is not done with Job, and his situation gets even more dismal.

Then Satan went before God a second time, devil that he is.

Then the LORD asked Satan, "Have you noticed my servant Job? He is the finest man in all the earth—a man of complete integrity. He fears God and will have nothing to do with evil. And he has maintained his integrity, even though you persuaded me to harm him without cause." (Job 2:3)

Defiant as ever, Satan sneered, "He blesses you only because you bless him.... Take away his health, and he will surely curse you to your face" (Job 2:4-5). So God gave Satan permission to touch Job's body, but he was not allowed to kill him.

Again, Satan acted quickly, and Job's entire body broke out in festering, itching boils. I can only wonder when the boils hit him if Job wished he could die. We aren't told, but surely it crossed his mind. He scraped his skin with a piece of broken pottery while he sat in the ashes. Mrs. Job watched their world caving in and could stand it no more. She had to speak. She just had to. This was so outrageous. She lashed out at her husband,

"Do you still hold fast your integrity? Curse God and die!" But he said to her, "You speak as one of the foolish women speaks. Shall we indeed accept good from God and not accept adversity?" (Job 2:9-10, NASB)

Rather than focus on what might have been, Job focused on what is: God gives. God takes away. God's in control. Fighting with him, being angry with him, speaking out against him will do no good. With all of his losses, Job's mind wasn't filled with thoughts of what might have been: *If only my livestock had been better protected. If only my herdsmen would have survived. If only my children had stayed in their own homes for dinner. If only...* Job just didn't go there. He mourned; he grieved and he trusted God for the future. As a result, he was able to move on. "Job lived 140 years after that, living to see four generations of his children and grandchildren. Then he died, an old man who had lived a long, good life" (Job 42:16-17).

Who would have thought it? Job found that there is life after great loss. Job could have sunk to a sulking low, blaming God and refusing to go on. After all, when you've lost it all, why bother to think about going on? Is there anything to look forward to? You'll never know until you go forward and find out. It doesn't mean that you won't grieve losses, but when your grieving is over, it is time to move on. Job could have had a whole list of what-might-have-beens, but he didn't. He just trusted God, and in the end, God restored his losses beyond measure.

> The LORD blessed Job in the second half of his life even more than in the beginning. For now he had fourteen thousand sheep, six thousand camels, one thousand teams of oxen, and one thousand female donkeys. He also gave Job seven more sons and three more daughters.... In all the land there were no other women as lovely as the daughters of Job. And their father put them into his will along with their brothers. (Job 42:12-13,15)

FOCUS ON WHAT CAN BE

Life is what it is. What might have been doesn't exist, so don't even go there. When you start to think about what might have been, the only healthy, life-giving response is to tell yourself, "This is a fantasy. It's a waste of time to think about it. It is a waste of breath and good spirit to feel sorry for myself or to second-guess myself. I need to move on." Hold on to this truth. What might have been is out of reach. You can't get there from where you are, no matter how much you want to!

So you have a choice. Will you stop going to the place of what might have been, or will you keep making yourself miserable by your frequent visitations?

Begin to move on by taking your heart cry for all that you have missed to the only One who can do anything about your losses or your life. God loves you and longs for you to lean on him. He will give you more than your what-might-have-beens could ever give you. He knows you, loves you, and has plans for you. Trust him. He knows where you have been, and he knows what you long for. He is God.

THREE

"THEY SAID" DOESN'T MAKE IT TRUE

Those who hear not the music think the dancers mad.

—ANONYMOUS

I don't know anyone who has escaped criticism. One way or the other, we all receive it from someone. That's just the way it is. The challenge comes in deciding what we are going to do with what has been said, because it's not what happens to us but what *we think* about what happens to us that matters. So if you hate to be criticized and think that criticism is absolutely the worst thing that can happen to you, then it will hurt you deeply and have a negative impact on you. On the other hand, if you decide that everyone is criticized and that's just the way life is, you can live in the reality that "they said" doesn't make it true.

I recently counseled with a young woman who had asked to speak with me about her life circumstances. I left that session thinking we had come to some good conclusions and that we had agreed on some good action points. But it wasn't long before I began hearing rumors she was spreading about how terrible our time had been, how awful my advice had been, and how hurt she was. All I could think was, *Were we in the same session?* This woman obviously viewed our time together quite differently than I did, and she was openly critical of me. Her harsh assessment of my counseling abilities left me with a choice to make. Would I wonder whether her judgment was true and stew over it? Or would I examine what had occurred and determine if there was any truth in what she was saying? I chose the latter because I have realized that just because "they say" doesn't make it true.

Even though we might agree with this maxim in our heads, sometimes we have a hard time living it out.

IF CRITICISM DEVASTATES YOU

No one likes to hear what critics may have to say, but there is a big difference between *not liking* their words and *being devastated* by them. If you lack self-confidence, you likely have a grid that has been bent toward taking everything personally. You will be more susceptible to believing everything "they say" about you. If you lack self-confidence, you'll have trouble being objective about critical things people may say to you. Your mind will automatically go into defensive mode, and you will feel driven to prove your critic wrong. That was Sheila's problem.

She sat across the table from me wringing her hands. "I just want to tell him that he is wrong about me. I need to explain why I did what I did."

The "he" was Sheila's boss, and what she had done was to mix up an important letter with another important letter by putting them in the wrong envelopes and sending them to business associates of her boss—and he was angry. The letters contained information about one of the parties that should not have gone to the other party. Her employer was irate and told Sheila that she was careless and incompetent and that she should be cleaning the office instead of running it. His remarks were cutting and uncalled for, and he said them out of frustration, embarrassment, and anger.

But Sheila took his anger and his comments very personally. When she talked with me, she wanted to make an appointment with her boss to explain why she had made the mistake. She was convinced that her explanation would make him understand. She had already told him she was sorry, but she wanted to give him more of an explanation in hopes that he would apologize for what he'd said to her. I told her that I didn't think her explanations would get anywhere with this man. He was upset over what had happened, and he really didn't care what the reason was.

But Sheila couldn't see it that way. She kept saying, "But if he just knew why this whole thing happened, he wouldn't be so angry." As we talked, it was clear that beneath Sheila's need to defend herself was a deep-seated fear that his words might be true—maybe she wasn't a good office manager, maybe she was a careless person. In her mind, if these things were true, then she had no value as a person. She had nothing to offer. She wasn't able to look at what had happened to see if his remarks had any bearing on reality. Even when I would remind her of her excellent performance reviews—both from this same boss and from her staff—she discounted them. She was giving this man way too much power.

Sheila finally wore herself out trying to think up justifications. She just could not keep on doing it. Of course, as could be expected, after she quit trying to prove herself right, as time elapsed, she discovered that the whole incident didn't matter to him as much as it did to her.

The need to be justified is human, but when your grid is bent, the need to explain yourself is huge. You think, *I must be thought of as right or I can't live with myself. I have to make others understand and acknowledge how right I am.*

Oftentimes a lack of self-confidence is tied up with a need to be liked. This, too, can block your ability to be objective about what "they say."

All of us want to be liked, but some of us have *the need* to be liked. Underneath this desire is the belief that "If someone is criticizing me, it must be because that person doesn't like me. And if that person doesn't like me, I must be an unlikable person." When your value as a person is tied up with a need to be liked, you won't be able to evaluate criticism objectively. Instead, just as Sheila felt driven to justify her actions to her boss, you will want to try to convince the person to like you. That almost never works.

When you want to be liked, your goal is to please everyone you come into contact with. If your goal is to please, and you succeed, then you feel good—for a while at least. The problem, of course, is that eventually you will do something that evokes another person's ire or frustration. It's impossible not to! The deal is, you aren't going to please everyone, and not everyone is going to like you. That's reality.

So what do you do?

WHEN YOU HEAR WHAT "THEY SAY"

If you struggle with "they said," you can take a proactive stance. This may require a huge paradigm shift for you, but often that's what grid straightening is all about. A straight grid allows the fresh air of truth to flow through to you, and though the task is hard, the payoff is wonderful.

When you encounter negative feedback about who you are or something you've done, you can choose to take the following grid-straightening steps.

Assume That You Are Liked

First, give people the benefit of the doubt. Instead of assuming they don't like you, assume that they do—until evidence proves otherwise!

I have determined to do this because when I believe that people like me, I behave in a more open, caring way. (I don't do this in a potentially dangerous situation. That would be airheaded! If I feel endangered, I'm wary. But if not, why shouldn't I assume that I am liked?)

This is half the battle. After all, you don't have to be defensive if you have nothing to defend. Even if you know that someone has a criticism, if you assume that they like you, you will be more open to hearing what they have to say.

On the other hand, not everyone will be happy with you—and you may never know why. When this is the case, it usually says more about the other person than it does about you. Remember how resistant Sheila's boss was? His response to what happened likely stemmed from some insecurity of his own. It really had little to do with what Sheila had done, which was why it was futile for her to continue talking to him about it.

So if I find out that the other person clearly doesn't like me, I remind myself of the truth that not everyone is going to like me—and that's perfectly okay. *It's perfectly okay not to be liked by everyone.* It is not the end of the world.

Consider the Source and Motive

Next, ask yourself, "Does this person have enough information to be speaking?" Sometimes people speak before they have the whole story.

Recently I was signing books at a large convention. Women were standing in a long line. They had to wait in line for quite a while, which meant they really wanted to be there! That felt good.

Then a young woman stepped up to the table and told me, "I really appreciated your message. I didn't think I would get anything out of it, but I did, and I want to ask you to forgive me."

Puzzled by her request, I asked, "For what?"

"I didn't want to hear you speak."

I asked her why, and she almost sheepishly told me, "I heard some women talking about you, and from what they said, I thought you wouldn't have anything to say."

I assured her that I forgave her and then I had to let it go. I had work to do. People will say a lot of things, and since I had no way of knowing the source of these comments—or even what had really been said—I chose to let it go.

Along with considering the source, we should consider the motive. Does this person seem to have construction or destruction in mind?

I was at another conference, and I almost heard what was being said about me. Because it was a big conference in a large auditorium, many in the audience had to sit far away from the platform, which hampered their ability to see the speaker's face clearly. After I spoke, I sat down at a table with several women. One of them leaned over and asked me, "What did you think of the speaker?" I have a mischie-vous streak and could have played along with her until she realized that *I* was the speaker, but I had mercy on her instead and said, "Be-fore you go any further, maybe you should know I am the speaker."

I still smile about that moment. My words hushed her up, and she couldn't get away from the table quickly enough. Her embarrass-ment told me she probably was more concerned about telling others what she didn't like about "the speaker" than with talking to me.

You can assume that you are liked, but you can't assume that everyone's motives are pure. That's why I always ask for God's help when I'm trying to discern the motives of someone who has given me some negative feedback. He lets me know whether I should take what has been said to heart or not. I hear him in my head gently persuading me to go one way or another.

You may not be able to discern a person's motives right away, but if you listen carefully, you'll be able to tell whether he or she is speaking out of concern for you or from some other motive. Some people have the "gift of correction" and use it just because they have it. Others genuinely care for you and are willing to risk the relation-ship for your sake. These are the people you want to listen to. If some-one is willing to risk your relationship because he or she loves you enough to tell you the truth, you can trust that that person has your best interests in mind. Listen to what is being said. Give yourself time to process it.

And if you've been hurt by what "they said," take your feelings to God.

Take Your Hurt Feelings to God

One of my favorite people in the whole world is Bible teacher Beth Moore. She says that when she hears something that hurts her feelings, she just tells God about it and then makes the decision to love. It helps to know that he understands how it feels to be misunderstood or disliked. If you are confident that God knows and understands, and that he will take care of it if necessary, then you can go on and live your life. This, by the way, is an art of living that takes practice. The more you take what "they say" to God, the straighter your grid becomes.

It may not be easy to believe that someone as big and powerful as God could care about you, but he does. You have a choice: Either believe him or not. Believe, you win. Fail to believe, you lose.

When God tells us, "I have loved you with an everlasting love; therefore I have drawn you with lovingkindness" (Jeremiah 31:3, NASB), he is talking about all those who want to have a relationship with him. When you take him up on his offer to save you from yourself and to make you into the person he wants you to be, you have his guarantee that you are loved with an everlasting love.

So for the rest of your days, you can assume that, no matter what, God loves you. Now that is huge. If he loves you, then you are a loved person, no matter what your present circumstances might be.

Ask for his help in acknowledging the following truths:

- I don't have to feel good to be all right.
- I don't need everyone's approval to be a person of value.
- I don't have to perform to get everyone's approval.
- I can hear criticism and still like myself and be comfortable with who I am.

If you've embraced these truths, you can weather the "they said" storm. That was certainly true for my friend Michelle.

Michelle is a gracious woman who seems to be a lightning rod for people's opinions. She is beautiful, married to the love of her life, and enjoying life—and this often intimidates those who don't know her well. Many people have a jaundiced belief that attractive, talented women are shallow and stuck-up.

She is a woman with many gifts who can do a lot of things well. She is warm and gregarious and seems to always know just what to say. She is also very creative. She can take a few tin cans, some flowers, and a little ribbon and make amazingly beautiful centerpieces. She has volunteered a number of times to help on different committees at church and at her children's school. Whatever they might want her to do, she is able and willing to do, but no one ever seems to want her on their committee. The excuses are always lame—"She is too emotional." "She is too creative. We just want help. We don't want her ideas."

But Michelle has handled rejection well. She knows her motives are good, and she is comfortable with who she is. Instead of trying to explain herself or getting angry and resentful because people have said negative things about her, she has moved on by finding things she can do to help without being on a committee. She is at peace with the situation because she knows she has God's approval.

Ask Whether It Rings True

Are you willing to look at the feedback and think it through, or does your grid immediately reject any criticism as unwarranted and unappreciated? If your grid slams shut whenever criticism comes your way, you may be missing out on some good stuff. Just because the things people say aren't necessarily true doesn't mean that the things they say are never true. Maybe you do need to change something. Maybe you do need to make amends, or maybe you just need to be aware that someone has an opposing view, and the two of you will never agree.

Take what "they say" to God and ask him if it is true. God could be speaking to you—even through an unlikely speaker. He may be sending you a message. What he says is right, and you can accept it as truth.

If someone who knows and loves you tells you something about yourself that is painful to hear, and you reject it out of hand or get defensive about it, then your grid is probably bent. Can you hear what is being said, or are you struggling with what this person must think of you because she is saying it? Do you have old tapes from your childhood that immediately start playing when anyone points out a perceived flaw in you? If you've asked God to help you replace these tapes, and they still are playing, you may need professional help. Seek it. Remember—*if something isn't working, change it!*

I have a friend who runs better on a calendar than a clock. She is habitually late and seems to have no sense of time. This has worked to her detriment, and many people who love her have told her this, but the words always seem to hit a button that, in her mind, makes comments about her time problem equal to saying something disparaging about her mother! She can't hear the simple truth for the roar of the old tape recorder switched on by a hair-trigger button. She doesn't say this aloud, but her response would indicate that tardiness has always been an issue. She seems to feel devalued, unappreciated, and threatened when anyone mentions her "late issues." She withdraws, appears hurt, and becomes defensive. Until my friend can recognize that this is old information and old feelings from old tapes, she'll continue to wrestle with feeling threatened anytime someone mentions her tardiness.

Respond Appropriately

If an answer is required, make sure your words are gracious, whether you think the criticism is valid or not. You can choose to maintain your dignity and good manners and treat the person with kindness, even if you have been treated harshly! I love this passage from *The Message:*

> I tell you, love your enemies. Help and give without expecting a return. You'll never—I promise—regret it. Live out this God-created identity the way our Father lives toward us, generously and graciously, even when we're at our worst. Our Father is kind; you be kind.
>
> Don't pick on people, jump on their failures, criticize their faults—unless, of course, you want the same treatment. Don't condemn those who are down; that hardness can boomerang. Be easy on people; you'll find life a lot easier. (Luke 6:35-37)

If you have discovered that you are wrong, have the grace to say, "You know, I think you are right about that one. I am so sorry. I was wrong. Will you forgive me?"

It takes a big person to say, "I'm wrong." It is tough to let go of your right to be right and be humble enough to admit you were wrong. Yet when you do, you will feel relief. When you find out that it's okay for you to be wrong every now and then, you'll be more comfortable in your skin. Since you don't have to live up to the image of always being right, you can relax.

IT'S ALL PART OF THE JOURNEY

Everyone who has ever walked on this earth has been criticized—even the only perfect person who ever lived. Jesus came to Earth to walk among us, to show us what the Father was like, and also to let us know he understood what it was like to live as we do, rubbing shoulders with difficult people.

No matter what Jesus did, he couldn't please the religious leaders of the day. If he healed, it was on the wrong day. If he ate dinner, it was with the wrong people. If he told the truth about himself, he was called a liar and a blasphemer. He knows what it feels like to take it on the chin, day after day.

He's been through weakness and testing, experienced it all—all but the sin. So let's walk right up to him and get what he is so ready to give. Take the mercy, accept the help. (Hebrews 4:15-16, MSG)

Criticism is a part of life. But just because "they said," it doesn't make it so. Remember that. And the next time "they say," take the mercy and accept the help that Jesus offers—and then keep on going. It's part of the journey.

FOUR

IF SOMETHING DOESN'T WORK, CHANGE IT

It is never too late—in fiction or in life—to revise.

—NANCY THAYER

Several years ago I owned an electric can opener designed to open tall cans. I used it often and became frustrated equally as often because the can opener did not function properly. In order to get it to work, I had to fight with it and jiggle it around a bit. Eventually, I would get the can open, but the opener was more trouble than it was worth. I hung on to it a lot longer than I should have, because I would think, *Well, it still works. I haven't had it that long. I'll get a new can opener the next time I'm at the store.* I procrastinated and spent many months getting exasperated because I didn't take my own advice: If something doesn't work, change it.

Eventually, a friend took pity on my plight and bought me a new can opener. It is simple and manual, and it works. It is easy to use and has not offered me a minute's frustration. I threw away the old can opener and celebrated the fact that I had eliminated one irritation from my life.

Doing the same thing over and over again without success is not smart. After a few times around, it's time to change the strategy. You may have the same goal in mind, but you need to find a different way to get there. Wisdom is the gift to see that good ideas are not always workable and that altering your approach is not defeat.

I wonder how many frustrating or heartbreaking events could be avoided if we had the courage to make a change when what we are doing isn't working. We are often so comfortable with the status quo (even if we don't like it) that change is the last option we consider.

Sometimes all it takes is being made aware of our need to change. In his book *Do One Thing Different,* psychologist Bill O'Hanlon tells the story of a former teacher of his, the late psychiatrist Milton Erickson. A favorite aunt of one of Erickson's colleagues had become severely depressed. Erickson was giving a lecture in the town where she lived, and his colleague asked him to look in on this aunt to see if he could help her. She was in her sixties, wealthy and living in a mansion, but she had never married, and she lived alone. She had medical problems that had put her in a wheelchair, so she rarely ventured outside her home. She was depressed and had thoughts of suicide.

After his lecture, Erickson went to visit the aunt. She met him at the door and gave him a tour of her home. The house was closed and depressing, that is, until she gave him a tour of her greenhouse. She came alive when she told him how she took cuttings from her African violets and started new plants from which she took more cuttings and started more plants. In the conversation that followed the little tour, the aunt disclosed that although she had this grand house and loved her greenhouse, she felt very isolated. She hired a man to take her to church on Sundays, but she always left early so she would not impede the flow of traffic after the service.

Erickson listened to her story and then told her about her nephew's concern about her depression. When she admitted she was seriously depressed, Erickson told her that the depression wasn't her problem—it was that she wasn't being a good Christian. The aunt was appalled at this thought and became defensive, until he explained,

"Here you are with all this money, time on your hands, and a green thumb. And it's all going to waste."[1] He then recommended that she get a copy of the church membership roll and the latest copies of the church bulletins. He told her she would see all the happy and sad occasions that were happening in the lives of the people in the church. He suggested that she make a number of African violet cuttings and put them in gift pots to give to the people who were experiencing the happy or sad events, along with her congratulations or condolences and comfort. When she heard this, the woman said that she would get right to work on his suggestion.

And indeed she did. She changed the way she had been living life and began distributing African violets all over town. In fact, when she died, the newspaper did a feature article on her with the headline, "African Violet Queen of Milwaukee Dies, Mourned by Thousands." The article detailed "the life of this incredibly caring woman who had become famous for her trademark flowers and her charitable work with people in the community for the ten years preceding her death."[2]

This woman changed just one small thing, and her whole life was revolutionized. Change can lead to the greatest life of all. If changing even just one thing can be so powerful, why do we resist it? What skews our grids so that we don't want to admit that something isn't working and that we need to make a change?

GUARANTEED TO SKEW YOUR GRID

Many people fail to make a change because of *fear*. Fear fills you with self-doubt, stealing your confidence. You focus on all the things that can go wrong, instead of admitting that what you have been doing isn't working. Fear prompts you to think:

- *What if I change what I am doing and end up in the same kind of mess?*
- *What if I change my behavior and my husband doesn't change?*
- *What if everyone thinks I'm crazy for putting down a sure thing and going for something that isn't sure?*
- *What if I didn't see things clearly and nothing was as bad as I thought it was? Maybe I am just imagining that things aren't working.*

It doesn't take long before we go right back to doing the things that weren't working. Let me explain.

A friend of mine and her elderly mother live together in my friend's home. The mother is strong-willed, and so, I would say, is my friend. They have daily confrontations over the remote control. The mother has a television in her room, but she prefers to watch the television in the den. She changes channels and talks through every show, which drives my friend crazy. Her mother picks up the remote as soon as she comes in the den where the family is, takes control of what is on the television, and starts her rambling commentaries. My friend has complained, fussed with her mother, and expressed frustration to all her friends, but she has never tried to resolve the situation with her mother.

When I suggested that she ask her mother to watch the television in her own room when she wanted to be in control of the remote, my friend rolled her eyes. She said her mother would not like it, and she wanted to avoid a confrontation. My friend was afraid of her mother's negative reaction. Ironic, isn't it? They were having regular confrontations anyway! They were stuck in a dance, and my friend was afraid to change the dance. Even though she didn't like them, their confrontations over the remote were familiar and predictable. She didn't know how her mother would respond to her proposal for change—and that produced a little fear that the shaky peace she now enjoyed would be disturbed.

Eventually, my friend mustered the courage to talk with her mom, and they were able to work out some rules for how to use the remote. They agreed that if the family was in the den, Mom would watch the television in her room. If the family was gone, she was free to watch the television wherever she wanted. That seemed to satisfy her. This change allowed them both to maintain a sense of power and yet also watch television the way they wanted to, with a little cooperation.

My friend's fears about her mother's reaction were unfounded, but that's not always the case. Sometimes we might start to make a change, but we give up at the first sign of resistance. Changing what isn't working can be like turning a rusty screw. It takes effort and initiative to budge something that has been set a certain way for a long time, and we don't want to expend that much energy. If other people resent it when we try to make a change, the ensuing conflicts can make us feel as though the changes we are making are wrong—even though they aren't.

That's what my friend Casey experienced.

I remember when Casey became acutely aware that her doormat attitude toward her husband, Bob, was destroying her and creating a monster of a husband. Bob had held the reins of control since the beginning of their relationship. Even then he had been jealous and dominating, but he also had some wonderful qualities. He was charming and entertaining. Casey was convinced that whatever happened, they could work it out, so she married him with her eyes half-shut.

Several years into the marriage, her eyes opened fully, and she realized Bob had been mistreating her and that she had been allowing his mistreatment. Casey realized she was stuck in a bad place. For instance, she had a part-time job that paid enough to have personal money, but Bob demanded that she dutifully hand it over to him. The checking account was in his name, and she had to ask him for money anytime she needed it—even to buy their groceries. She had to tell Bob how she would spend the money and give him all her receipts so that he could double-check her spending habits. Then he would lecture her as if she were a twelve-year-old if she failed to do what he thought was right. But now she had had enough. She was no longer willing to live like she had been living. She didn't want to leave Bob, but she didn't want to continue allowing him to control her.

Through counseling, prayer, and a lot of introspective thought, Casey realized that she had traded her personhood for Bob's approval. So she determined that she would continue to be his wife and honor him as her husband, but she would not live as an oppressed woman. She opened her own checking account without his permission and began depositing her paychecks into that account.

Bob wasn't happy about his loss of control. He pitched a few "Bob" fits and tried to punish Casey for making her choice to change, but she stuck by her decision and let him deal with it. She had learned that it wasn't her problem if her husband didn't approve of everything she did. It was his. He would have to find a place to land. Bob didn't like that his wife was changing, and he kept telling her that he liked the relationship as it was before. After all, he had the upper hand! Why wouldn't he like it?

Some days Casey thought, *It is just too hard! I feel as if I am doing something wrong.* She continually had to back up and see the big picture of what was going on in their relationship. She had to remind herself that Bob's attempts to control her life weren't limited to money. He spoke disparaging remarks about her almost from the first month of their marriage and had outbursts of anger every time she came up with an idea that he didn't like. She knew she had to change the way she responded to his unreasonable demands or she would lose herself completely. She had to challenge his selfish behavior.

If you try to change and meet with resistance, you're faced with a tough challenge. You may want to throw up your hands and quit, but remember why you are initiating the change: What you are doing isn't working.

YOU NEED TO MAKE A CHANGE WHEN...

You Aren't Meeting a Desired Goal

When I was in college, I had a professor who said the craziest thing and yet it made sense. "There are more ways to choke a cat than hot butter." I spent many classes mulling over how a cat could be choked with hot butter. Of course, I knew he wasn't really speaking of a cat. He was making the point that there is more than one way to do something. And, indeed, that is true. If you have tried to reach a goal and failed, perhaps you should look at another way to go about achieving it. For instance:

- If you hate your job, get a new one.
- If you have failed at losing weight, take another approach. Maybe you need to count carbs or fat instead of calories.
- If you want to have more time, get up an hour earlier.
- If you want to master the piano, take lessons.
- If you want to learn sign language, take a class or at least read a book.
- If you want to exercise but don't have time, walk up and down your stairs several times in a row. It's a start!

There are many ways to achieve a goal. You just have to look for them…and then be willing to pay the price. Sometimes, the change is so important that you have to do whatever it takes to bring about the alteration. That's what my parents did.

They were poor, depression-era kids who met, fell in love, and married. They lived in a place where the work opportunities were very limited. They wanted more for themselves and for me, and they knew that staying at a dead-end job with no hope of getting ahead was not going to give it to them. So when I was two years old, they decided to pull up stakes and move to Washington, D.C., which at that time was a city of opportunity.

They made the move and rented a one-room apartment, even though neither of them had jobs. In the corner of the room was my bed made from two overstuffed chairs that had been pushed together.

It was winter, so we kept milk on the windowsill and ate all of our meals at the little restaurant down the street.

My dad walked the streets, looking for a job with the government, which he eventually found. My mother wanted to be with me, but she also had to work, so she began looking for a job in a child-care facility, which would enable her to do both. She was offered a job at a day-care center and worked there until I started school. By the time I had to go to school, she had her teaching certificate. I attended the school where she taught until I went to junior high school. In fact, Mom was my fifth-grade teacher.

My parents paid a price to change their lives, but it was a price they were willing to pay, because in the end they believed they would gain more than they gave up. Such is often the case.

You Feel Frustrated About What's Happening

You should also consider making a change if something continues to cause you frustration and irritation.

I have several black pieces of clothing that will shrink if they are put in the dryer and a husband who does the laundry as often as I do (if the truth be known, probably more often). Sounds wonderful, right? Most of the time it was—except when my once full-size black top suddenly appeared in my closet as a tiny black top.

I knew what was happening. Charlie was doing laundry the way he had always done it. Wash it, then dry it. I hated to say anything to him because I didn't want to discourage his industrious ways, and I didn't want to do all the laundry again, either. We had a good thing going. At first, I just tried to accept that I would have one or two shrunken black tops every time Charlie did the laundry. But the problem was, I couldn't keep replacing them. So instead of insisting that he change how he washed my clothes, I told him, "Honey, if it's black, don't touch it, okay?" That was fine with him. Ever since then he washes everything but my black clothes, and I see that they get the proper care.

If something is making you frustrated, you can either make peace with it, or you can gracefully work to change it. For instance, if you are dealing with someone who is chronically dissatisfied with the food at any restaurant, ask her to pick the restaurant. If she acts demure and says, "Oh no, you pick," tell her, "I'll do it on one condition, and that is you won't find fault with the food." Before you tell me you couldn't be that direct with your difficult person because it would make him or her angry, hear me out. Here's the deal. One of you is going to be upset—you or your difficult person. Who's it gonna be? Make a decision. Is it worth the effort of trying to change?

God Is Being Dishonored

Anytime God is being dishonored by dishonesty, lack of integrity, immorality, or just plain rebellious, sloppy living, you need to make a change.

Scripture tells the story of Deborah, who became a judge in Israel at a time when women were not judges. People brought their disputes to her, and she held court. She loved her people and reverenced her God.

Her people were in a difficult time. Sisera, the commander of the army of the Canaanite king, Jabin, had oppressed them for twenty years. The Canaanites not only oppressed the Hebrew people, they also opposed their God. One day, God told Deborah that this oppression had gone on long enough. So she sent for Barak, the commander of the Israelite army, and told him what God had told her. God wanted Barak to assemble ten thousand warriors and guaranteed that he would lure Sisera to the Kishon River and give Barak victory. That sounded good to Barak, but he said he would not go unless Deborah saddled up and went with him.

Deborah agreed. I don't think that was her original intention, because God had told her to tell Barak about the battle plans, and they didn't exactly include her. But she was willing to do something unheard of for women because this was a huge deal. God was being opposed, and he had had enough. Deborah didn't stand on decorum and say, "Well, women don't go to war." She took the challenge, defied the culture, changed her plans, and told Barak she would go with him. But she made it clear he would not be coming back a big hero.

> "Very well," she replied, "I will go with you. But since you
> have made this choice, you will receive no honor. For the
> LORD's victory over Sisera will be at the hands of a woman."
> (Judges 4:9)

Indeed, she did go with him, along with ten thousand warriors. They marched together down Mount Tabor to get in the face of Sisera's army.

While that was happening on one front, another woman was

getting ready to bring about change, and some pretty dramatic change at that. Jael lived in a tent by a large oak tree not far from where the big battle was coming down.

Everyone could feel the tension in the air, I'm sure. Barak and his ten thousand were approaching Sisera and his boys, who had the coolest kind of iron chariots. I'm sure that when you are in an iron chariot going up against people on foot and on horseback, it would never occur to you that you could be defeated. But when it became obvious that those chariots weren't worth a flip against Barak and Deborah's boys, Sisera and his warriors panicked. Sisera, being the brave commander that he was, took off running…right into the arms of a woman who was waiting in a tent by an oak tree. (While he was leaving the scene of the ambush, I might mention, all of his men were killed.)

When he reached Jael's tent, she said, "Come in. Don't be afraid" (verse 18). So, thinking he had found refuge, Sisera came in and lay down, and she covered him with a blanket. He asked for water, but Jael went the extra mile and gave him milk—warm sleep-inducing milk. (Nothing like the hospitality of a woman with a mission!)

"Stand at the door of the tent," he told her. "If anybody comes and asks you if there is anyone here, say no" (verse 20). Obviously, Sisera believed this little woman was going to do exactly what he said, but was he in for a surprise!

"But when Sisera fell asleep from exhaustion, Jael quietly crept up to him with a hammer and tent peg. Then she drove the tent peg through his temple and into the ground, and so he died" (verse 21). All Jael had to do now was wait.

Barak came looking for Sisera. He knew the commander of the opposing army had to be somewhere close to the battle. And indeed he was. Jael was waiting to show her contribution to the change that was coming down. So she invited Barak in to see Sisera lying on the floor with a tent peg through his head. Imagine the double take Barak did when he saw his archenemy pinned to the floor in such an undignified fashion.

Both Deborah and Jael had what it took to embrace change. Deborah had already displayed her willingness by becoming a judge in a male-dominated society. Still, marching into an actual battle probably took all the courage she could muster. We don't know as much about Jael, except the girl knew how to use a hammer and a nail!

I'm sure there were plenty of women during that time who had experienced the enemy's oppression. No doubt they thought things never would change. They got up every morning sighing and went to bed at night weeping over the fact that that terrible king was giving them fits. Finally, two women were in a position, by God's appointment and their willingness, to bring that whole oppressive, godless kingdom down.

I wonder how many of us are sighing in the morning and weeping at night because something in our lives needs to change. Perhaps it's the way you relate to a family member, or it's your financial situation, the kids' school circumstances, or your mother-in-law. Such things can give us great grief. If something needs to change, why not change it? If it's not working now, why not draw up the courage to alter the situation? You are not alone, although sometimes it may feel as if you are.

THE ONE YOU CAN COUNT ON

"Whatever is good and perfect comes to us from God above, who created all heaven's lights. Unlike them, he never changes or casts shifting shadows" (James 1:17).

When you are faced with change, you'll be much more successful if you can rely on God's wisdom and strength. Change can be challenging, particularly if you are correcting long-held beliefs or long-established relationships.

People may change the way they relate to you because you have changed, and it may not be pretty or feel very good.

Your church may not embrace you because you have changed. They may not understand your new freedoms or your new depth of spiritual commitment.

You may face some losses you didn't count on because you have chosen to change.

Change is risky, that's for sure, but if you know something isn't working, it is riskier to stay on the same path.

There is great risk of things deteriorating further.

There is great risk of passing the dysfunction on to the next generation.

There is just great risk.

That is why you can count on the only One who never changes. He is always the same and is there for you with a steady presence.

When the children of Israel were getting ready to enter the Promised Land, Moses reminded them of God's promise: "Be strong and courageous, do not be afraid or tremble at them, for the LORD your God is the one who goes with you. He will not fail you or forsake you" (Deuteronomy 31:6, NASB).

He went with them.

He never failed them or abandoned them.

The same will be true for you.

If something needs to change and you know it, wisdom says it's time to draw up your plans. What will it take for you to change? What will you have to believe before you are willing to undertake the change? Who will you need to call on when the going gets rough?

God will walk with you as you take the first step.

FIVE

FRETTING ONLY
DESTROYS YOU

It's hard to fight an enemy who has outposts in your head.

—SALLY KEMPTON

I caught myself fretting not long ago. I was driving my grandchild to her kindergarten class, and we were running late. Problem was, we kept running into roadblocks—literally. I had tried several different routes, and each of them was blocked. This was getting frustrating. When I turned down the final road and saw that it, too, was blocked, I got really annoyed. I pulled my car behind some orange barrels to ask a policeman if he had a suggestion for an alternate route. To my surprise, he barked, "No. You'll just have to go down Jenkins Road."

Well, Jenkins Road was *not* where I wanted to go. It was way out of the way. So I said, "I know this is not your fault, but this whole thing is a big mess."

He immediately jumped on me, saying, "Just be glad I didn't arrest you for driving behind *my* orange barrels."

I immediately thought, *His orange barrels? I believe since I'm a taxpayer, they might be just as much my orange barrels as his. And what does he mean he'll arrest me? For what? I asked a question for heaven's sake. That's all, and now he wants to arrest me? Not in America. I don't think so.*

I was tempted to remind him that as a taxpayer, I paid his salary, and if I wasn't transgressing the law, he was not authorized to throw his weight around! But instead of losing what cool I had left, I turned my car around and headed for Jenkins Road. While I was turning, Officer Orange Barrel threw in a little more insult. "Don't run over my toes, lady!"

Grrrrrrr! The man had made the whole thing personal. I really hate it when people twist the truth like that! It flies in the face of what is right. I was spittin' angry. I kept telling off Office Orange Barrel in my head, but I'm happy to say it didn't last long. With a few seconds of sane contemplation, I decided to let it go. I knew I could do nothing to change what had happened, and fretting over it would serve no purpose.

In this instance, it wasn't that difficult to let go of what had happened and move past my anger. But that's not always the case, particularly if you have been deeply wronged or if you see someone getting away with something that is destructive or downright evil. The more grave the injustice, the more apt we are to fret, to replay it over and over again, all the while getting more and more angry.

WHAT'S SO BAD ABOUT FRETTING?

Today, most of us think of fretting as worrying. We might tell a mother, "Don't fret so much about whether your kids will turn out. Do what you can and trust God with the rest. You can't control what happens anyway, so what good is worry?" *Fretting* usually refers to an inability to let go of anxious thoughts. But in ancient times, *fret* often meant more than that, as we see in the following psalm.

Do not fret because of him who prospers in his way,
Because of the man who carries out wicked schemes.
Cease from anger and forsake wrath;

Do not fret; it leads only to evildoing. (Psalm 37:7-8,

NASB)

In this psalm, *fretting* refers to a worry that is fueled by anger, particularly over those who are getting ahead by wicked schemes. But we don't just fret over those who get away with murder, we also fret when we aren't getting where we want to go or getting what we want to have, and we are upset and worried about it—worried with an edge. We are worried in such a way that our annoyance shows. Our worry has a sharp, you'll-get-yours sort of air about it.

Fretting is the dark side of worry. Worry is anxiety over something—a sick child or an estranged sister or a job situation that is unstable. You can worry and not be angry, but you cannot fret and not be angry. When you fret over something, you are not only deeply anxious and concerned about it, you are mad.

The truth is, when you worry and obsess out of anger—when you fret—it can destroy you. Fretting changes nothing and can deprive you of sleep and rob you of peace. Fretting has no redeeming value. It can begin with annoyance and irritation and turn into rage. It is a burning anger that sits in the pit of your stomach and causes irritation. The anger associated with fretting isn't an explosive, in-your-face kind of anger. Although that kind of anger is destructive in its own way, it's not fretting. The anger that comes with fretting lies just beneath the surface. It is a helpless agitation, like the obsessive gnawing of a dog tormented by fleas. You focus on what is wrong, you think about what is wrong, you mull over what is wrong, you figure out how to fix what is wrong—and you go back to thinking about what is wrong. Chew, chew, chew.

Fretting consumes and destroys you. Let me explain.

When I first met Sonya, it didn't take long to learn that her father had walked away from her mother and her family and was living a life of ease. This rubbed a sore into Sonya's soul. She seemed to be angry, hurt, and obsessed all at the same time. Every conversation with her ended in a harangue about her father's selfish and despicable behavior. How on earth could he get away with having all the money he wanted while her mother and family were barely able to make ends meet? Sonya had tried her best to get her father to change by telling him how his reprobate behavior was creating such a hardship on the family. But he was unmoved, letting Sonya know that he couldn't care less about her mother's tears. The fact that his family was barely able to keep a roof over their heads and food on the table meant nothing to him.

When Sonya wasn't able to convince her father that he was wrong, it only made her fret more. After all, what her dad had done was wrong! He was wrong! Sonya made sure that everyone knew the truth: *Her dad was wrong!* But fretting over the fact that her dad was wrong—and getting away with it—did not change the facts. Facts are what they are. More than that, Sonya's fretting over her dad's wrongs hurt her. It made her unhappy, unpleasant to be around, and unable to go on with her life. That's what fretting does. It destroys.

Wisdom says: Let it go. "Do not fret because of evildoers" (Psalm 37:1, NASB). "An unjust man is abominable to the righteous" (Proverbs 29:27, NASB).

FATAL FLAWS THAT FUEL FRETFUL ANGER

When we feel envy and jealousy, a sense of entitlement, or anger over injustice, we have a hard time letting go. In fact, each of these feelings can fan our smoldering pile of fretting into a red-hot flame.

Envy and Jealousy

Envy and jealousy may cause more fretting than any other emotion. Jealousy says, "I don't want you to have what you have," and envy says, "I want what you have." They turn into fretting when you say, "Why you and not me?"[1]

Put envy and jealousy together with anger, and you have fretting. "I don't understand why you and not me, and I am really ticked off about it and can't get past thinking about it—a lot. I don't like this feeling, but I don't like what has happened either."

Almost two decades ago I cohosted a radio program. At the time it was unique because two women hosted it. We had a good idea and put a lot of work into making the program a success. Unfortunately, two and a half years into the program, the two of us decided that it would be best to go our separate ways. The travel that I had to do in order to participate in the program was wearing on me, and several other factors made it clear that it would be best if I moved on, which I did.

I left slightly wounded and began to fret a little over the way things had happened. Then three months after I left, the program was nominated for a very prestigious award. I am ashamed to admit that the envy and jealousy I felt turned my little bit of fretting into big-time fretting. I was angry because I wouldn't be getting the award, and I was equally upset that my former cohost would be. This was not okay with me. I wanted that award too, and I deserved it! What kind of deal was this? We had both worked hard on making the program what it was, yet I wouldn't be there to receive the recognition, and my contribution would not be acknowledged. (This, at least, was how I believed the whole thing would be handled.)

Up until the night the award was given, I chewed over how unfair this was like a dog gone mad over a flea! I was hurt, incensed, agitated, angry, ashamed, and in a hotheaded fret. I hated what I felt, but I hated what was happening to me. Fretting had me in its grip.

I look back on this time in my life and think, *What a waste of energy.* It changed nothing and only made me tense, irritable, and worn out.

Fretting—for whatever reason—is miserable. It makes you feel small and embittered. Not a way to be.

A Sense of Entitlement

Another fuel that stokes the fire of fretting is the modern malady of entitlement.

It has seeped into our twenty-first-century American psyche that we are entitled to certain things, and it's awful if we don't have them.

Erica is a gifted young writer who came out of an atrocious background. Her parents were both neglectful and abusive, and when Erica left home, she felt that life owed her. She had suffered enough, and it was time for her to get a break. After all, she was due—long,

long overdue. All her friends told her how exquisite her writing was—and it was—and she figured it would be easy to secure a contract. But that didn't happen. Erica sent out what seemed like hundreds of manuscripts, only to have them returned with rejection notices. She felt angry that publishers would print drivel yet kept rejecting her material, which she knew was far superior.

As Erica fretted, she directed her fury at God. She knew enough about him to know that he could do what he wanted to do. So why was he holding out on her, especially now? Her grid had a huge bend in it that said, "If you have had a rough life, you are entitled to God's intervention to make you successful." She knew God was good, and it seemed a good thing that he would take her case under advisement. Maybe he would even give her added blessings because she had tried to be good. She prayed and gave money to the church, so where was God when she needed him? Erica's sense of entitlement increased her feeling that she was being treated unfairly by everyone, including God.

When you have been hurt and offended on an ongoing basis, your grid can be bent into thinking that the world owes you something. The whine can become deafening and the grid unyielding. "Why have things turned against me? Why am I not getting what I think should be getting? Is God holding out on me?" Yada-yada-yada.

Here's the deal. This belief exonerates you from all responsibility and puts your success in someone else's court. Nowhere is it written that you are entitled to success. Nor is God at your beck and call. If you are fretting because God's not coming through the way you want him to, lay it down. Give it up. Let it go.

Anger About Injustice

Do the same if you are angry about injustice. While anger about injustice can be good and right, when we hold on to our anger and it turns to fretting, we are in trouble.

John and Beth hired a Web designer to do some work for them. He promised to deliver a Web page that would rival anything on the Internet. He was full of big promises but was less than forthcoming about the hidden costs he had slipped into their agreement. When they saw the finished product, they were dismayed. Their Web page would rival anything on the Web all right. It was about as bad as or worse than any Web page they had ever seen. They were upset. He had done a terrible job. It failed to represent them well and was just plain shoddy.

They contacted the designer to express their disappointment and suggest how the project might be salvaged without an increase in the fee. In what should have been a civil conversation, he became vindictive and threatened to sue them. John and Beth could not believe his irrational, bilious remarks. At first they thought he was just having a bad day, but two weeks later they began to hear that he had e-mailed negative press about them. They knew then that they were dealing with an evil man who was out to get them.

Soon their irritation over his bad behavior turned to anger and fear. They began to fret over what he might do to them. *How far is he going to take this? Since we signed an agreement, will we have to pay for this job, even though we can't use it? What will he try to do to our reputation? What was really behind his threats to sue? Could he possibly have a case? Will we have to hire a lawyer to take care of this guy?* Their peace was disrupted, and their lives were in turmoil.

Finally, they realized the unjust designer had the upper hand because of the fine print in their contract. He had them. They had to pay money they didn't have to get rid of a man who wouldn't leave their lives without a fight. Where was the justice in that? John and Beth could have stewed for a long time over what had happened, but you know what? It wouldn't have gotten them a good Web design. It wouldn't have paid their bill. All that it would have done was make them more angry and unhappy. That's what fretting does.

You don't have to live with fretting, but to stop fretting, you need to see your worry and anger for what they are. They don't change the situation, they only destroy your peace. Wisdom says lay them down.

SO HOW DO YOU STOP FRETTING?

Remember You Aren't in Control—and You Never Were

The deal is, you won't stop fretting until you learn one of the great lessons of life: "I'm not running the show. I am participating in it, but I am not running it."

To stop fretting, take a cue from David. When he was young, he ran up against a situation that would have made his teenage knees knock with fear and his valiant heart beat with anger, a perfect situation for fretting—yet he didn't. It happened like this.

The Philistines had stationed themselves on one mountain, and the Israelites had positioned themselves on another. The taunts flew back and forth between the two armies, but the Philistines seemed to have the upper hand, or at least the biggest mouth! His name was Goliath, and his size was legendary.

> He was a giant of a man, measuring over nine feet tall! He wore a bronze helmet and a coat of mail that weighed 125 pounds. He also wore bronze leggings, and he slung a bronze javelin over his back. The shaft of his spear was as heavy and thick as a weaver's beam, tipped with an iron spearhead that weighed fifteen pounds. An armor bearer walked ahead of him carrying a huge shield. (1 Samuel 17:4-7)

This incredible specimen of humanity had a cruel heart and impure motives. He represented those who hated God and God's people. Goliath struck fear wherever he walked. He could have been the Osama bin Laden of his day. Who on earth could deal with this nine-foot monster?

Well, there was one young shepherd who showed up on the scene, and as ridiculous as it seems, he took on the big boy. He didn't get caught up in worry because his grid wasn't muddied with old fears and anger. When David saw what was happening on the battlefield, he was angry. *Who does Goliath think he is to come against the armies of the living God? Huh?*

When King Saul found out that David wanted to fight the giant, he looked at the boy and said, "You are too young and Goliath has been bred for war. He has been at this game a long time."

But David said to Saul, "I have had some experience you don't know about. I was taking care of my father's sheep when a lion came and took a lamb from the flock. I took out after him and tore into him and I ended up rescuing that lamb. I took it out of that lion's mouth. Then I grabbed him by his scruffy beard and hit him and I killed him."

And David said, "The LORD who delivered me from the paw of the lion and from the paw of the bear, He will deliver me from the hand of this Philistine." And Saul said to David, "Go, and may the LORD be with you." (1 Samuel 17:37, NASB)

David was angry at Goliath's audacity, but he had to be a little fearful as well. Yet he didn't give in to fretting. Instead, he remembered how God had delivered him in the past. He refused to succumb to fretting.

We all know the story. David picked up five smooth stones from the brook. He put them in his shepherd's bag, took his sling in his hand, and did the only thing that makes fear flee. He approached the object of his fear. He went toward the Philistine—and nailed him in the forehead with a stone. But notice what he told Goliath beforehand:

This day the LORD will deliver you up into my hands, and I will strike you down and remove your head from you. And I will give the dead bodies of the army of the Philistines this day to the birds of the sky and the wild beasts of the earth, that all the earth may know that there is a God in Israel, and that all this assembly may know that the LORD does not deliver by sword or by spear; for the battle is the LORD's and He will give you into our hands. (1 Samuel 17:46-47, NASB)

Talk about a clear grid. David knew who was in charge, and he was not going to put up with that big-mouthed Philistine.

David didn't have time to fret over the fact that he was just a kid who knew how to tend sheep or that this guy had everyone quaking in fear. He knew he had done some pretty tough things before and God had been with him then. He had no doubt that God would be with him when he went up against the giant. And he was.

To stop fretting, change your focus from "what if, what if, what if" to "God, I'm afraid that this might happen, but you are in charge of the universe and can make all things right. This is wrong, wrong, wrong, but you can make it right." If, like David, you have gotten through some tough situations, you may have some history to go on. If not, start building that history now. It will stand you in good stead in the future.

Commit everything you do to the LORD.
Trust him, and he will help you....
Be still in the presence of the LORD,
and wait patiently for him to act.
Don't worry about evil people who prosper
or fret about their wicked schemes.
Stop your anger!
Turn from your rage!

Do not envy others—

it only leads to harm. (Psalm 37:5,7-8)

Face Your Anger and Deal with It

All of us are going to be angry at some point. There is nothing wrong with anger that is handled wisely. I have always found the best way to deal with anger is to look at it for what it is. Am I angry because I am hurt or because I feel rejected or disappointed—or what? Anger always has a trigger.

For instance, let's go back to the run-in I had with Officer Orange Barrel. My angry response to him was rooted in an event that had happened several years before, when another police officer who was guarding a grocery store gave me a ticket for parking in the handicapped zone. My mother's car had a handicapped sticker on her license plate, and I had parked in the space because she was with me. We had gone into the store to get a few groceries late on a Saturday night.

When we went back to the car, we were surprised to see the ticket. Sure that there was a mistake, I went back into the store, found the policeman at the entrance, and with a broad smile, said, "I know this is probably a mistake because I have a handicap sticker on the tag." He turned away from me and said, "I've already written the ticket. You will have to go to the courthouse."

I followed the officer and said, "But I have the right handicap sticker." He immediately said, "Get out of my face. And if you don't pay that ticket, you will get a hundred-dollar fine." I could not believe my ears. I was angry.

As a result of his intractable stand, I had to drive downtown to the main courthouse, take the ticket and the handicap sticker to the traffic division. They dismissed it immediately, but it had taken the better part of my morning to deal with it. The incident was over, but there was a little pocket of anger that joined up with feeling misunderstood and ignored that resurfaced as fretting later on.

When Officer Orange Barrel took the same kind of attitude, it triggered my anger and started me fretting. If I didn't want to continue fretting, then I had to get over my anger. When I realized what was making me so angry, I was able do some grid straightening. *Yes, this man was rude to me and treated me unfairly, but where is it written that life is fair? This situation is not the end of the world, is it?* I realized that if I allowed myself to dwell on my anger and fret, it would hurt me. It would make me feel worse, not better.

One of the best maxims I have learned about anger is found in the Bible: "*Be angry, and* yet *do not sin;* do not let the sun go down on your anger" (Ephesians 4:26, NASB, emphasis added).

Anger has to have a boundary. The best way to stop it is to bring it to a conclusion. Let it go before it destroys you.

Take a Proactive Stance

Instead of fretting, assess the situation and do what you can to move forward. We can all find things to fret about. That's easy. It's harder to stop it before it starts—but it can be done! When you feel yourself beginning to fret, you can:

- Ask yourself, "What am I really feeling? Worry? Anger? Envy? Jealousy? Do I feel entitled to something? Am I angry over an injustice?" Sometimes fretting is so much a part of how you operate that you don't even understand what it's about.

- Once you have identified what you are feeling, ask, "What can I do about it?" There are times when there is something you can do. If you think you know what it is, do it. If you can't do anything about the situation, remember you aren't in control. God is good to everyone, and he would like to help you with the things that bother you.

- Determine that you are not going to remain angry for long. Stop it within a twenty-four-hour period. Deal with it or drop it. Life is too short for protracted anger and all of its little hateful friends—envy, jealousy, and entitlement—that keep fretting alive.

- Stay away from people who habitually fret. Fretting is contagious. You don't need to be around anyone who has the habit. It only will draw you right back into the swampy mess you have escaped.

- Don't allow yourself to fret aloud. Back up and talk to yourself: "Fretting only leads to destruction. I don't want to be destroyed, so I turn from fretting to a healthier mind-set."

- Challenge your grid. My friend Sally sent me this e-mail a few months ago:

Why does everything that means anything to me just slip away? I always wanted to be married, and now I am divorced. I wanted to have children, and I could have only one, and she's grown now. I always wanted a career in teaching, but every time I tried to finish school, something happened to prevent it. I even found a church I like, and about the time I got involved, the pastor had an affair and left. Upheaval one more time! I could go on and on.

Well, I couldn't let her grid go unchallenged. Yes, she'd had some disappointing things happen, but there are many events in a lifetime, and not all are disappointing. I wrote back and asked Sally to list all the good things that had happened in her life. For a long time, I didn't hear from her, then she sent a few lines and said, "I'm working on it, but I'm still mad."

"Fine," I said. "Keep working. At least you are challenging the bends in your grid."

That's what it takes.

Are you a fretter? If so, you have a choice. You can continue to let the problem eat at you, or you can let it go and take away its lingering power in your life. What's it going to be? You get to decide.

SIX

DON'T TELL EVERYTHING
YOU KNOW

There are things to confess which enrich the world and things that need
not be said.

—JONI MITCHELL

It was a night to remember. The fourth-grade boys at my church were having a banquet with their moms. I was the speaker. Having raised three boys myself, I knew I had to move quickly and keep their attention. The topic was "Words." The illustration was feathers. I offered a twenty-dollar reward to any young man who could collect all of the feathers I was pulling out of a pillow and tossing around the room. They were excited and so was I. The more they scrambled to get the feathers, the more feathers I pulled out of the pillow until we had a veritable feather storm.

Despite the chaos, I made my point. Words are like feathers. If you let them loose, you can never get them all back. You may recover some, reclaim some, even sweep some under the rug, but you can never get them all back.

Of course, that point was brought home even more clearly to me after the boys and their moms went home. Someone had to clean up all those feathers. Several of us worked for a long time, but we never did pick up all the feathers scattered around. They were stuck and hidden in places we would only discover in the weeks and months to come.

Just as we couldn't gather up all those feathers and put them back into the pillow, it is impossible to take back words once they have been said. So be prudent before you say anything. Realize how powerful your words are. Think about where your words could lead. We can't control what someone does with our words, and if we aren't wise about what we say and why, what we say may come back to haunt us.

ONE MAN WHO TOLD TOO MUCH

Just ask Samson. He could give us a lot of insight in his hindsight. You'll find his story in the book of Judges. He had a major feud going with the Philistines. He married one of their women, and then he left to attend to business. Later, her father double-crossed Samson by giving her away to Samson's best man. When Samson returned to claim his wife, he discovered the betrayal. Enraged, he tied the tails of three hundred foxes together in pairs, set them ablaze and let them lose in the Philistines wheat fields. Samson and the Philistines had a vendetta going now. They killed Samson's wife and father-in-law. In retaliation, Samson single-handedly killed one thousand Philistines with the jawbone of a donkey.

Samson ruled Israel for twenty years before he fell in love with another Philistine woman, Delilah. The Philistines saw their chance to move in and get even.

> The leaders of the Philistines went to her [Delilah] and said, "Find out from Samson what makes him so strong and how he can be overpowered and tied up securely. Then each of us will give you eleven hundred pieces of silver."
> (Judges 16:5)

Obviously, Delilah was a gal who enjoyed silver, liked a challenge, and didn't mind being obvious. She sweetly asked Samson what made him so strong and what it would take to tie him up securely.

Well, he played along not once but three times, each time telling Delilah some ridiculous tale about how he could be bound. He made fun of her by leading her on a wild goose chase. Each time, she followed his instructions, and the Philistines would come and try to overpower him. Finally, we read:

> Then Delilah pouted, "How can you say you love me when you don't confide in me? You've made fun of me three times now, and you still haven't told me what makes you so strong!" So day after day she nagged him until he couldn't stand it any longer.
>
> Finally, Samson told her his secret. "My hair has never been cut," he confessed, "for I was dedicated to God as a Nazirite from birth. If my head were shaved, my strength would leave me, and I would become as weak as anyone else."
>
> Delilah realized he had finally told her the truth, so she sent for the Philistine leaders. "Come back one more time," she said, "for he has told me everything." So the Philistine leaders returned and brought the money with them. Delilah lulled Samson to sleep with his head in her lap, and she called in a man to shave off his hair, making his capture certain. And his strength left him. Then she cried out, "Samson! The Philistines have come to capture you!"

When he woke up, he thought, "I will do as before and shake myself free." But he didn't realize the LORD had left him. So the Philistines captured him and gouged out his eyes. They took him to Gaza, where he was bound with bronze chains and made to grind grain in the prison. (Judges 16:15-21)

Delilah's nagging wore Samson down, despite his better judgment. I have no doubt that in hindsight, Samson would loudly declare, "Don't tell everything you know; it could come back to haunt you." Be careful when you are tired of a topic or become weary in a confrontation. You may be tempted to say things you wish you never had said. You also need to be careful about who you tell things to. Samson apparently ignored Delilah's obvious connection with the Philistines—or else he had such an inflated view of himself that he didn't believe he would really lose his strength if she cut his hair! Either way, he chose to tell his greatest secret to someone who was untrustworthy. Big mistake.

GRID-STRAIGHTENING GUIDELINES

If your grid keeps you from knowing when to speak and when to keep silent, here are some guidelines:

Check Your Motives

Before you speak, check your motives. Why do you say what you say? Have you ever stopped to listen to yourself and wondered, *Why am I saying this? Do I have a good reason that will be helpful to someone along the way, or am I talking for my own benefit?* If you listen to yourself talk, you will hear your motives tripping out on your words. Anytime you are tempted to name-drop, gossip, or gain the upper hand, you'd best keep silent. Your motives are out of whack.

Avoid Name-Dropping

People love to know the scoop on someone of note. That's why a really good gossip columnist can make a decent living. If you tend to name-drop and tell what you know about other people because you think it makes you look good, beware. Your grid is bent and needs straightening. You may feel a little more important if you can say you know someone important, but the good feeling is short-lived because we don't really receive any true value from what we know. What really counts is who we are! If you know who you are and what you are about, it doesn't matter if you hang out with the queen of England or the little waitress at the corner diner. You are you and they are they and you are all just folks. (Yeah, even the queen. She's got the jewels and the palaces, but she's got family struggles just like a lot of other people. She is just who she is.)

I have been a friend of Kay Arthur of Precept Ministries for over thirty years. (I'm not name-dropping here, trust me. I'm just trying to make a point.) It is amazing what people have asked me about her. "Does she really cook?" "Where does she get all those beautiful clothes?" But the funniest question was after Kay had written in one of her publications that she had sat on my deck. Someone came up to me several months later and asked, "Did Kay Arthur really sit on your deck?" I had to smile because I could have told her, "Yes, and she ate at my table and opened my refrigerator and visited my bathroom." But rather than bait this woman any further, I just smiled and said, "Yes."

If I told everything I know about anyone in my life, especially those who are in the public eye, that would be a violation of the relationship. The safest people are those who don't have to know something, nor do they talk about what they do discover.

There is a certain glory in keeping your mouth shut.

Don't Gossip

When you do open your mouth to speak about someone else, even when making a prayer request, ask yourself, "Does this really need to be said, or am I revealing personal information?" Unless you have that person's permission, you are gossiping when you tell someone else's sad story—even if it's only a prayer request. I hate the word *gossip,* and I hate the connotation that goes with it even more, but I wonder how many times I have been guilty of this contemptible habit just because I knew something and felt compelled to tell it.

When my lips get too loose, I often turn to the book of Proverbs. It is a great place to visit to get your grid straightened when it comes to knowing what to tell others. "A gossip goes around revealing secrets, but those who are trustworthy can keep a confidence" (Proverbs 11:13). Sadly, a gossip usually feels free to tell other people's secrets. None of us wants anyone telling our secrets, but we often tell someone else's personal information without another thought. "A gossip tells secrets, so don't hang around with someone who talks too much" (Proverbs 20:19). That's a fairly direct injunction. So obviously, when you hang around with people who talk too much, it's easy to pick up the habit. Don't.

Don't Abuse Your Power

Another reason we tell what we know is that we think it gives us the upper hand. However, if you think knowing something makes you somebody, you are in need of more than information. Don't fool yourself, friend. Knowing something others might like to know is like having more money than someone else has. If you are classy, you keep the information to yourself and pull out the money only if you want to bless. If you have nothing to prove, then whatever you know, you have no need to tell it unless it is appropriate.

Don't Say Too Much Too Soon

This is a good rule of thumb. One of the biggest relational mistakes you can make is telling too much too soon to someone you just met. Rushed intimacy will bring more regrets than carefully considered openness. Getting to know a new person in your life takes time. You don't have to be afraid of intimacy, just be wise. Wisdom isn't aloof and standoffish. It doesn't put up walls and isolate itself. It takes things one step at a time when it comes to getting to know someone. It gives every relationship time to develop.

What you see at first in anyone is not always what you will see later on. Time and truth eventually reveal the core nature of a person. So be careful with what you reveal to someone you haven't known very long. You don't want to have the anxiety of having said too much. That can only leave you with regret.

Once you get to know the core of a person, you can make the decision to tell something about yourself that is intimate—or not! You will never regret what you *did not* tell when you discover that the person you thought you could trust is a little less trustworthy than you thought.

After hearing me speak on this topic, one woman wrote to me, saying, "My dad often said that my mom never had a thought she didn't share, and I'm a lot like that." She went on to say that it had never occurred to her that maybe she shouldn't share personal things with others right after meeting them. She had grown up thinking that revealing personal information about herself was what she needed to do to make other people feel comfortable. She thought she was being "real."

All of us want to be thought of as real, but being authentic doesn't mean telling it all. Being real means being honest and true to who you are; it means not misrepresenting yourself. It doesn't mean telling the intimate details of your life. What you see is not always what you get, so be very careful what you say and to whom you say it.

Honor Family Members and Friends

Of course, even if you have a close relationship with someone, and that person has proven to be trustworthy, be careful what you reveal about family members and friends. It is a wise practice to keep your spouse's, your children's, and your friends' personal issues separate from your own. This is even true about things you may not mind someone telling about you. Let me give you an example.

I have absolutely no problem with those who take antidepressants. I think these drugs are a wonderful gift to our generation. Many people have found miraculous relief through taking them. Unfortunately, there is still a stigma related to their use. One of the couples I worked with several years ago almost came to a standoff in their relationship when the husband found out his wife had told her mother and best friend that he was taking an antidepressant. He was furious, humiliated, and embarrassed. His wife was dumbfounded by his reaction. "After all, Momma and Carol aren't going to tell anybody. You know that." No, he didn't know that. But more important, he didn't want Momma and Carol to know this information about him.

So even if you have no problem with what you are getting ready to divulge about a family member or friend, think it through. The person you are talking about may have some real issues with your open discussion of his or her business. Everybody has a right to his or her own business, and someday the shoe may be on the other foot, and you will want your friend, your spouse, or your child to keep a zippered lip!

It is a matter of honor to refrain from telling everything you know. It honors your family and the safety that family should give!

Sadly, some families, under the guise of family honor, hide a lot of dirty little secrets and harmful behavior behind closed doors. That is obviously not what I am talking about here. If someone is being hurt by the silence, that silence should be broken.

You should know that:

- Legally you are required to tell if you believe a child is being abused.
- Legally you are required to tell if you are aware that a crime has been committed.

In addition, I believe you are morally bound to tell if you are aware of an immoral situation. You are at least required to go to the one who is being immoral with what you know.

A few years ago a good friend of mine, whom I'll call Donna, became aware of a mutual friend's plan to leave his wife and marry a younger woman. Through a bizarre set of circumstances, a person doing business with this man gave Donna facts about this man's indiscretion. Because Donna truly cared for the man and his wife, she called his office and made an appointment to see him. She told him she knew what he planned to do and asked him if it was true. He immediately denied it, but before she could return to her office, he was making frantic phone calls, threatening to sue the person who had revealed his plans. Donna heard him and turned around, went back to his office, and said, "I know it's true. I am so grieved."

She opted not to go to his wife, having told him that she knew. She felt she had done all she could to bring him to his senses. The end of the story is not pretty and really irrelevant. What people decide to do with the truth is not our responsibility. It is our responsibility to speak the truth to the one who can do something about it. (Again, I reiterate, *keep your own counsel unless you know someone is in danger.* Then you shout what you know from the rooftops. Insist that you be heard, and keep shouting until someone takes you seriously.)

Don't Give Advice Unless You're Asked

God makes it clear that wise people will listen to advice and have advice to give.

> People who despise advice will find themselves in trouble;
> those who respect it will succeed.
> The advice of the wise is like a life-giving fountain;
> those who accept it avoid the snares of death. (Proverbs 13:13-14)

Wise people, however, know when to give advice and when to keep it to themselves. Not everyone is anxious to receive what could be a life-giving fountain, and unwanted advice can backfire on you. Best wait until you're asked before you dish out your words of wisdom. This especially is true of parents with adult children. Once you no longer have authority over your kids, you no longer hold responsibility. Nor do you have a captive audience for your advice. Once they are grown, it is wise to ask permission to give any pearls of wisdom.

I like what one of my close friends tells her adult children, "If you don't mind me giving you advice, I don't mind if you don't take it!" She truly doesn't mind if they don't do what she has suggested, because she at least has been able to offer them help. After that, she leaves it with God.

If you feel you must tell your kids your opinion and offer them your advice—and they don't want it—you will put up a wall in your relationship. Let me be blunt. Even if they are doing some really ill-advised things, DON'T DO IT unless you know they will welcome it. Instead, pray about it, and keep your mouth shut unless asked. Advice about big things will most likely only be received if it is asked for.

Sandra's son Allan had always been strong-willed. From the time he was a little guy, he liked to call his own shots. Sandra knew this about her son and had learned how to deal with him. But when he brought home a girl who Sandra had real reservations about, she made the mistake of telling him her misgivings about his girlfriend's character, as well as her doubts about the girl's ability to be a good wife to him. Sandra went further than she intended to, but she felt such concern for Allan's future that she told him all her reservations.

Her words came back to haunt her when Allan reacted in anger and told his fiancée what she had said. Sandra is now the mother-in-law of the daughter-in-law from hell. She says, "I have bent over backward trying to love her, give her things, and make her part of the family, but she will have nothing to do with me, and Allan has pulled away. When he makes one of his rare visits, he brings his wife, who may or may not come out of the bedroom to eat with the rest of the family. Allan excuses her and blames me for her behavior."

Sandra lost her son to a woman she knew was trouble. Had she not said so much, she may have been able to have a positive relationship with her son and his wife. It is hard to know, but still she wishes she had remained silent.

I am the mother of three adult sons. As they aged, the scales that had been weighted in my direction because I was the parent were slowly being weighted in their direction as they became self-governing and responsible for themselves. I no longer have the responsibility or the right to give unsolicited advice that once I had. Now, I consider my words very carefully. It is my responsibility to be careful about what I say. I don't want my advice or even my casual words to come back to haunt me because they have hurt our relationship.

Get Permission Before You Tell Your Spouse

I have known people who have felt obligated to share other people's secrets with their mates, simply because they are married. This perspective, the result of a bent grid, will cause problems. A perfect example of this is Peg, a pastor's wife who told her husband about some counseling she had done with a woman in the church. The counseling was of a deeply personal nature.

The next week when she met with the woman, Peg mentioned what her husband had said when she told him about this woman's problem. The counselee was horrified. "You didn't tell him, did you?"

Peg replied, "Of course, I tell my husband everything, and he tells me everything." The woman became very upset and began to cry. "You didn't tell me you were going to tell him! I am so ashamed. I can't show my face in this church again." And she didn't come back. Peg was grief-stricken. She had never had a second thought about telling her husband everything, but this dear woman's response brought her up short.

Clearly, if the individual wanted to tell her heart secrets to both Peg and her husband, she would have asked to speak to them as a couple. This experience helped straighten Peg's grid on this matter. She apologized and asked forgiveness, but the deed was done. The feathers could not be recalled. It was too late to prevent the woman's pain, but at least Peg determined not to make that mistake again.

Nowhere is it written that spouses must tell each other everything they know. That really is a form of codependency. Just because you are married doesn't mean you share a brain. Just because you are best friends doesn't mean that if you know it, your spouse has to know it too.

There is an unspoken code of ethics that I believe is applicable to everyone. If you are privileged to know someone's personal information (something that person would not freely share with someone else), you do not have permission to share it with anyone else unless that person has released you to tell it.

What If You Have Committed Adultery?

Whenever I speak about not telling too much, someone always comes up afterward and asks, "What if you've committed adultery? Shouldn't you tell your spouse?" I will say right up front that *there is no one answer to this question.* However, if you have been indiscreet and have been discovered, the best thing to do is confess and live with the consequences. If you are asked if you have had an affair and the answer is yes, then of course you have to confess your wrongdoing.

But what if you had a one-night stand, feel terrible about it, have confessed it to God and repented, and have had no further contact with the person? Should you tell your mate what you did? You are almost certain that your spouse will never find out, but you feel guilty, and you don't know what to do.

DON'T TELL EVERYTHING YOU KNOW

If it's highly unlikely that your spouse will ever know what happened, and you have never committed adultery before and are committed never to do so again, I advise you to think carefully before speaking. If you tell, what will you accomplish? You will have rolled your burden over to your mate, and what will that do but cause pain and suffering? If there is no clear redemptive purpose, then why hurt your spouse? If you don't tell, then you will have to live with your guilt, which is uncomfortable, but your mate will be spared unnecessary heartache.

I have seen two marriages ripped apart because one spouse confessed his or her infidelity. No one would ever have known, but both of the offending parties felt they must tell their spouse. Both felt that telling their mate would relieve their guilt, but it did not. It only enlarged the circle of offense. Unfortunately, the spouses could not handle the revelation, and both marriages ended in divorce.

I'm sure many will say, "But, Jan, that's not honest." I am not saying that every situation is the same. Whether you tell or not is ultimately a personal decision, but I am saying you should think before you confess something that may devastate your mate.

It's just a thought. I hope that you will never need to consider what to do about such a situation, but if you do, please think before you speak.

THERE IS A TIME TO SPEAK

As we've seen, the power of the mouth is like the power of a loaded gun. If you don't know how to use it, it can be deadly at the worst and

101

messy at the very best. Most of the time, we're tempted to say far too much. There are a couple of exceptions. We've already noted the times when you are legally bound to speak. You should also speak up to defend someone's reputation, to protect those who have no protection, or to cry out against injustice.

The Scriptures say, "*Speak* up for those who cannot *speak* for themselves; ensure justice for those who are perishing. Yes, *speak* up for the poor and helpless, and see that they get justice" (Proverbs 31:8-9, emphasis added). Wise people know when to speak, what to say, and to whom to say it.

I have a good friend who has come alongside someone who has had no one to speak for her. In fact, she has had more people speak against her than anyone I ever have known. To speak out for her is costly and in many ways injurious, but my friend has set her face like flint to be unwavering in her support and unmovable in her confidence. She has made the choice to speak for this woman, even if it comes back to haunt her. That takes a measure of courage that only God can give. And that is why some extraordinary women are making some bold, costly statements without fear.

One of these is a dear woman I know who, at the age of sixty-three, decided she will speak out for the poor, afflicted prostitutes in a poverty-stricken Third World country. She has spoken by offering them cool water, a roof over their heads, a simple occupation to get them off the streets, and a place for their children to stay. She has spoken, and whether it comes back to haunt her or not, it matters very little. She has a mission and a heart as big as Texas.

So remember, don't tell everything you know. It may come back to haunt you. But speak when you must and have the courage to stand on what you believe.

SEVEN

FEELING GUILTY DOESN'T MEAN YOU ARE

It is quite gratifying to feel guilty if you haven't done anything wrong: how noble!

—HANNAH ARENDT

When it comes to feeling guilty, my friend Bobbie is Everywoman. Most of her life she has carried around a lot of guilt—sometimes over an actual wrongdoing and sometimes not.

When she was young, Bobbie had two abortions. She had them willingly and without remorse. Years later her guilt surfaced. When it did, she felt it deeply and knew that she had to do something about it. She couldn't bring back her babies, but she could acknowledge that they had been conceived and had lived in her womb a few weeks before they died. She did some recovery work in a group with other women who had similar experiences, and she was finally able to accept God's forgiveness for what she had done. She also had a memorial service for her unborn children and has since been able to lay aside her guilt over the abortions.

After Bobbie had the abortions, she married Rob. Bobbie likes to make men happy, so she worked overtime trying to make Rob happy. Meanwhile, he was having affairs and becoming more and more hostile toward her. When the marriage blew apart, Bobbie found herself sitting on the side of life's road, blaming herself for their divorce. Some people who knew nothing of the situation suggested that if she had been more attentive, cooked better meals, had more sex, then Rob would not have been involved with other women. They told her it was her responsibility to hold the marriage together. She took their words as gospel truth, and so she felt the divorce was her fault.

I met Bobbie several years later when she was working at a beauty salon as a manicurist. One day while she was doing my nails, Bobbie overheard me talking about spiritual things with someone sitting near her station. I said, "You can know you are acting in opposition to God when you have that sort of sick feeling inside when you do things that are wrong, such as lying." Out of the corner of my eye, I saw Bobbie noticeably stiffen. Later I would find out why.

A few nights earlier, Bobbie had borrowed a coworker's flatiron for straightening hair. When she finished using it, she dropped it, and it broke. Horrified, she put it back but didn't leave any note of explanation. Sure enough, when she arrived at work the next morning, her coworker asked whether she knew what had happened to the flatiron. Bobbie immediately denied knowing what had happened and went on about her business.

A few days after that incident, she overheard my comment about lying. Conviction—what I would call "good guilt"—poured over her. She was visibly shaken. She excused herself, went to her coworker, admitted what she had done, and offered to pay for the flatiron. She came back to her station, liberated and breathing freely. She had been convicted of her deception, she had done what she could to make things right, and from that point on, she no longer lived under condemnation.

Like many women, Bobbie felt guilty when she was guilty, guilty when she wasn't guilty, and guilty because someone else told her she should feel guilty. She is the perfect illustration for the point of this chapter: Just because you feel guilty, it doesn't mean you are.

The purpose of guilt is to motivate you to right your wrongs. So when Bobbie asked God to forgive her for aborting her children and her coworker to forgive her for taking and breaking the flatiron, she received forgiveness and was freed from her feelings of guilt. However, she couldn't find the same freedom over the guilt for her divorce, because she hadn't done anything wrong and could do nothing to make her guilt go away. This is "bad guilt." Bad guilt keeps you in a place of helplessness, with no relief in sight. Bad guilt hangs around your mind, pops up front and center from time to time, and does a real number on what you think of yourself.

Are you like Bobbie? Is your grid bent toward feeling guilty— whether you've done something wrong or not?

DO YOU STRUGGLE WITH BAD GUILT?

Do you ever feel guilty when…

- Someone asks you to do something, and you tell them no because you are too busy?
- You have already planned to give your money to a specific cause, but someone else makes an appeal for money, and you feel as though you should give to him or her, too, but don't really want to?
- Everyone seems to like the speaker, but for the life of you, you are totally unimpressed?
- Someone expresses disappointment in you?
- You think of all the things you could have done for your kids but didn't?

If so, you struggle with bad guilt.

I haven't met a mother yet who didn't feel some bad guilt for what she didn't do for her children when they were small. It's that problem of not being perfect. Of course, none of us did everything we could, and that's why we feel guilty. I still experience guilt from time to time when I think of opportunities I missed with my boys. I was young when they came along, and all I knew to do was what I did, but now there are so many things I would do differently. I watch my daughters-in-law with their little ones, and I admire how they handle their children so patiently and so well. I think of the times when I was pre-occupied with what I wanted to do, and I feel guilty.

My sons are pretty laid back, and they kid each other and me with great glee. Recently they were sitting around my kitchen table, talking with some friends who had joined us for dinner. The boys had an audience, so they began talking about their childhood and life with Jan. I, of course, was within earshot, so they embellished their tales pretty well. One said, "She didn't let us have toys. We played with spoons in the yard." Another said, "Yeah, that's right, our toys just kept disappearing, so we used the spoons." I waited to see what kind of dramatic statement would follow this when the oldest one said, "Yeah, and I heard we had another brother, too, but well, he disappeared." At that point we all started laughing, and I remembered why I love my boys so much.

How do I know that what I feel is bad guilt? Because I have talked to my sons about the things I wish I had done for them, and they look at me as if to say, "What's the problem? You were our mom. We grew up. No big deal." They can't offer me forgiveness because they have nothing to forgive. I think I felt bad guilt over my parenting just because that seemed the motherly thing to do.

Can you identify? If you struggle with feelings of bad guilt, they likely stem from your childhood, when most of your grid was formed. You may have grown up hearing guilt-producing messages similar to these:

- If you were a better child, your daddy wouldn't drink so much.
- If you hadn't chased your brother, he wouldn't have fallen and broken his arm.
- I can't trust you to do anything right! If you had been more careful, you would not have put that dent in your mother's new car.
- You drive me crazy! If you were more like your sister, you wouldn't get into so much trouble.
- You don't think of anyone but yourself! How can you be so selfish?
- If you don't behave, Mr. and Mrs. Hornbecker won't let you come over to visit them anymore.

The list of guilt-inducing messages goes on and on, bending your grid so that, like my friend Bobbie, you feel guilt for things over which you have no control and hold no responsibility.

WHEN YOU FEEL OVERLY RESPONSIBLE

Being responsible is a big deal to me, which is often a good thing, but sometimes it makes me feel guilty when I'm not. For instance, I feel guilty for not keeping in touch with everyone who might want to keep in touch with me. Ever felt that way? You met some people on a family vacation, and you vowed to keep in touch? You got along well, and now you can barely remember their names, and you have a nagging sense of guilt. No one is telling you that you should feel this way; you do it to yourself—you know that you could be in touch with those people if you really wanted to, and the fact that you don't makes you feel guilty.

My overdeveloped sense of responsibility sometimes causes me to feel guilty for not doing things that I feel I should do, such as setting the table for Sunday dinner or cooking my husband a birthday cake from scratch. When I married, I felt guilty because I didn't can fruit like my mother-in-law did. I didn't want to can, my husband didn't care if I canned, I didn't know how to can, and we didn't have a need for me to can, but somehow I thought I should be canning because my mother-in-law canned. When I let go of that expectation, I discovered that my family couldn't tell the difference between jelly from the grocery store and jelly made from scratch anyway.

Many of us work up a load of guilt because we don't volunteer to do things. When you hear yourself saying, *I really should be doing that,* and yet everything within you cries, *No, I really don't want to do that,* you are feeling guilty about something that wasn't yours to feel guilty about. Not everything is your job, your calling, or your responsibility. I have to tell myself this grid-straightening message every time I see a stray puppy. I have this overwhelming feeling that it is my duty to take care of every one of them. *If I don't take that little puppy, who will?*

I know, I know. I need to listen to my own message! But I am telling you how it is with me—and I can talk myself into feeling guilty about a host of things.

We can even talk ourselves into feeling guilty because we have things that others don't have. I am really good at that. I can see people in great poverty and somehow work my way into feeling guilty for what I have. Just recently I was in a Third World country. I visited orphanages where the children wanted to be held and rocked, just like my grandchildren at home—but these children didn't have someone to rock them to sleep every night. They didn't have someone to give them hugs and kisses "just because." While I did what I could during the little time I spent with them, when I left, I felt guilty for leaving, for not doing more.

I have a friend whose mother is in a nursing home. She is semi-aware of what is going on and spends her days in a routine that breaks my friend's heart. She feels devastated that her mother is in this situation, but when her mother says, "I wish you could stay with me," my friend melts into a heap. Her mother doesn't mean to make her feel guilty, but my friend feels guilty because she can't take away her mother's loneliness. She feels guilty about something she can't do anything about.

WHEN OTHERS ACCUSE YOU OF BEING GUILTY

Many people use guilt as a way of punishing or manipulating others. You know the type—the mother who tells her grown children that they don't come see her often enough, or the friend who keeps reminding you of the time when you accidentally dropped and broke her favorite glass bowl.

Several years ago I decided it was time to leave the organization I was working for and go out on my own doing something similar to what I'd been doing. Several months later I ran into a former colleague and told her what I was doing, and she snapped, "If you can live with yourself and do that." Whoa! Back up the dump truck and unload the guilt. Her angry tone shocked me. I had never dreamed that my going out on my own would be an issue with this person. Obviously, she was more agitated over my leaving than I had perceived, and her words were intended to hurt me and make me feel as if I'd done something wrong.

However, this was one time when I was looking at the situation through a straight grid, and I knew I was being "guilted." All my attempts to find out why she said what she said were rebuffed. I told her I was sorry she felt the way she did. (Notice I didn't apologize for leaving, but I did acknowledge her feelings.) When she continued to refuse to talk with me about what she was really feeling, I made the choice to give her some slack and let her words—and the guilt they carried—roll off my back.

Because we can't control what others say to us, whether it is intentionally guilt producing or not, we have the responsibility to determine if we feel guilty because we have done something wrong or because our grid is bent.

How can we tell the difference?

FEELING GUILTY DOESN'T MEAN YOU ARE

WHAT TO DO IF YOU FEEL GUILTY

It's one thing to identify bad guilt when reading examples in a book. It's another to see it in your own life. Here's the best tool I know of for helping to identify whether the guilt we feel is good or bad.

When these feelings come, ask yourself this question: "Have I actually done something wrong?"

Every time the guilty feelings return, ask yourself again: "Have I actually done something wrong?"

Be honest. Your grid will never change until you honestly evaluate why you feel what you feel and do what you do.

If you can answer no, then you can move on with freedom. But if you answer yes, you need to make right what you have done wrong.

Here's the deal. God created us to feel guilt when we do something wrong, so that we would be prompted to do something about it. So if you ask yourself whether you've done something wrong and the answer is, "Yes, I have," then the guilt you are feeling is good guilt.

Good guilt is a sign that we have done something wrong and need forgiveness—forgiveness from God and from those we have wronged. When we receive forgiveness, our guilt is lifted and we can go on in freedom. This truth is repeated over and over again in Scripture.

One of the most compelling illustrations of this is seen in the life of David when he was king of Israel. We'll pick up his story during a time when he stayed home while his armies were on the battlefield. In those days, you could take a walk on the rooftops because they were flat. So one morning, David took a walk on his roof. He looked over at the roof next door and saw a beautiful woman, Bathsheba, taking a bath. That was all it took. David, the king, had to have her. Well, he got her all right, and as a result, she became pregnant.

David then had to cover up what he'd done because Bathsheba's husband, Uriah, was away at war. David sent for Uriah to come home, thinking that if he did, surely he would sleep with his wife and there would be an explanation for the pregnancy. But Uriah was an honorable man. He was the commander of men who were at war and couldn't come home, and he didn't feel he should have the privilege of a conjugal visit if his men couldn't, so he did not sleep with Bathsheba. He slept on the king's doorstep instead.

As you might expect, this whole thing got more and more complicated. David had to do something about this pregnant woman, so he sent Uriah to the front of the battle so that he would be killed. That would fix it. He would marry Bathsheba, and the little family would live happily ever after. End of story, right?

Wrong. It wasn't going to work that way. Uriah was killed, but God had other plans for David, whom he loved yet would not let get away with murder. God sent in a prophet. Now prophets were not known for their comforting words. They were the tell-it-like-it-is people of the day. So the prophet Nathan went to David and told him a story about a little lamb that lived with a poor family who cared for it and loved it. The lamb was their little pride and joy. Then a rich man, who could have taken a sheep from his own stock, took the poor family's little lamb and killed it to feed a guest.

David was enraged at such selfish greed. He immediately declared what should happen to such a callous fellow. You can imagine the dramatic silence when David finished passing judgment on this "selfish, compassionless" man. Nathan the prophet turned to David and said, "You are the man." David was stunned but knew that he had been found out.

David had slept with another man's wife.

He was guilty of adultery.

David had sent the woman's husband into the heat of battle to be killed.

He was guilty of murder.

So he did the only honorable thing he could do.

He confessed his sin, and although there were dire consequences, he received God's forgiveness and became free from guilt.

In fact, David wrote a poem that expresses the joy that comes when our guilt is forgiven:

> Oh, what joy for those
> > whose rebellion is forgiven,
> > whose sin is put out of sight!
> Yes, what joy for those
> > whose record the LORD has cleared of sin,
> > whose lives are lived in complete honesty!
> When I refused to confess my sin,
> > I was weak and miserable,
> > and I groaned all day long.
> Day and night your hand of discipline was heavy on me.
> > My strength evaporated like water in the summer heat.

Finally, I confessed all my sins to you
and stopped trying to hide them.
I said to myself, "I will confess my rebellion to the LORD."
And you forgave me! All my guilt is gone. (Psalm 32:1-5)

David had experienced a great truth: *No matter who you are or what you have done, if you confess your sins to God, you will receive forgiveness.* You are no longer guilty—the guilt has been washed away in the cleansing water of forgiveness.

If we claim that we're free of sin, we're only fooling ourselves. A claim like that is errant nonsense. On the other hand, if we admit our sins—make a clean breast of them—he won't let us down; he'll be true to himself. He'll forgive our sins and purge us of all wrongdoing. (1 John 1:9, MSG)

If you have done something wrong, you have to admit it, deal with it, and move on. That's what God wants for you.

Sadly, peace still eludes some people—those who say they know God has forgiven them, but they just can't forgive themselves.

BUT I CAN'T FORGIVE MYSELF!

If you feel this way, you have condemned yourself to feeling guilty— unnecessarily and for a very, very long time. *You will never be able to forgive yourself because it is not within your power to do so.* Think about it. How can you offer forgiveness to yourself? You weren't the person who received your offense, so how can you be the one to offer forgiveness? No wonder you feel frustrated! You are trying to do something that makes no sense and is an impossibility! Only God and those you have wronged can offer you forgiveness. The person you have hurt can send your offense away. God can send your offense away. But you cannot send your offense away. That is not your privilege. That's what makes this forgiveness thing so humbling. Only the one we have hurt or offended can give us this gift. We simply have to stand there and take it. It's pretty black and white. You can't forgive yourself, so you don't need to keep trying.

So the next time guilt comes knocking on your door, respond wisely. Ask yourself, "Have I done something specific that I know is wrong?" If the answer is yes, get rid of your guilt by repenting (changing your mind and your position), confessing (agreeing with God) that what you have done is wrong, and then accepting the forgiveness that is freely offered to you. If the answer is no, then ask God to help you straighten your grid by embracing this truth: *Just because you feel guilty, it doesn't mean you are.*

EIGHT

THERE IS A GOD,
AND YOU ARE NOT HIM

I have lived a long time, and the longer I live, the more convincing proofs
I see that God governs in the affairs of men.

—BENJAMIN FRANKLIN

If you took a poll of our country, most Americans would say that they believe there is a God of some kind. In fact, if you try to take God out of the Pledge of Allegiance, you'll get a fight from a good number of us! But while most of us may agree that God exists, where that belief takes us and how it affects our lives can be very different.

For instance, some people put God at the center of their lives, saying, "There is a God. I worship him and try to live my life in a way that pleases him." Others casually talk about God and say, "I believe in God, and we coexist peacefully. He doesn't bother me, and I don't bother him."

Additional comments about God may include:

- "I believe there is a God, but I'm not sure what that means."
- "There is a God, but I don't trust him, and I'm not sure he likes me."
- "There is a God and I trust him, but I don't understand why he has done so many harsh things, like killing all those people in the Old Testament."

Despite the differences in these views about God, all agree on the most critical point. All agree that *God exists*. If this is true, then it means that Someone besides us is in control of the universe. It is the very nature of God to be at the top of the heap and in control of what happens. People have known this since the beginning of time. Eugene Peterson writes,

But the basic reality of God is plain enough. Open your eyes and there it is! By taking a long and thoughtful look at what God has created, people have always been able to see what their eyes as such can't see: eternal power, for instance, and the mystery of his divine being. (Romans 1:21, MSG)

The irony is that even though we say we believe there is a God—and may even claim to know him—many of us haven't quite caught on to the reality that not only is there a God, *but* I am not him. It is easy to say, "There is a God," but it kills us to admit that we aren't the One in charge of the universe, calling the shots, deciding outcomes, and making all things right (as we see them), and so we often act as if we are.

Not sure you agree? Not ready to admit that you may sometimes play God? Well, stay with me. If you do not embrace the reality that there is a God, and you are not him, you will have an inflated view of your own power. See if any of the following telltale signs are true of you.

YOU TRY TO CONTROL OTHERS

People who have an inflated sense of their own power believe that they can control other people. As a result, they often tell others what they should and should not do. They use the words *should, ought,* and *must* to make others feel guilt, obligation, and condemnation. For instance:

- "You should call your mother. She is expecting to hear from you."
- "You should write a thank-you note immediately. The Smiths expect that, you know."
- "You must give Harriet a call. She is so lonely."
- "You really ought to mow that lawn for Henry."
- "You should know what I like. Why can't you be like other men who know what their wives want for a gift?"
- "You should be more careful with your sister's feelings. She has always been fragile."

The use of the words *should, ought,* or *must* make these legitimate statements sound obligatory and demanding. When you use these words, you are passing on your sense of what is right to another person, insisting that he or she should feel the same way. When you do this, you are imposing your will on another and taking a godlike position. In *Telling Each Other the Truth,* William Backus writes:

God gave ten commandments. But we human beings have discovered how to multiply them—by using obligation statements inappropriately to put others and ourselves under the law. These statements make our wishes sound like God's commandments, putting others under obligation to perform for us. We create a social climate in which people are chafing under the burden of, not ten commandments made by God for our good, but ten-to-the-tenth power commandments cooked up by others—with a lot more where those came from.[1]

When we play God, we try to manipulate others in order to get our own way. We want the person to feel obligated to do what we say. We can have all kinds of ideas about how other people should live their lives, and we do our best to force them to comply.

Most people will refuse to do what we suggest unless we are gracious about it. The healthiest way to approach people is as one human talking with another. You have no more power than anyone else, so it is important to ask in a kind, straightforward manner for whatever you want. For example, the previous statements could be rephrased:

- "It would mean a lot to me and be so kind of you if you would call your mother. She loves to hear from you."
- "The Smiths are always so pleased to hear when they have scored on a gift. If you get a chance, be sure to let them know what you think about the golf shoes they sent."
- "Harriet is so lonely. I called her yesterday. If you have a chance, would you mind calling her tomorrow?"
- "It would mean so much to Henry if you would mow that lawn for him. He hates being laid up after his surgery. He's not expecting it, but if you could do it, it would be a great surprise for him."
- "Honey, I don't expect you to know what I like. Why should you if I don't tell you? I'll give you a list any day you want it."
- "Your sister looks up to you as her big brother. Every word you say is important to her."

If you are going to make a straightforward suggestion, be prepared for a straightforward response. You can ask friends or family members to do something, but it is their prerogative to say no. If they do, then that needs to be okay with you. You may struggle with their response, but since you are not God, you acknowledge that they have the right to refuse your request. That's just the way it is, and that's okay.

YOU FEEL OVERLY RESPONSIBLE

An exaggerated sense of your own power can also cause you to feel overly responsible—as if you are indispensable. Without you, the project will fail, the show won't go on, and the party will be a dud. Everyone will be upset, and they won't be able to function without you. Wow. That's power. Sorry to pop your balloon, but this simply isn't so. No one is that powerful or important.

Last year I had to cancel three speaking engagements. In twenty years of speaking, I had never done this, but last year I got sick, literally and figuratively. I hated to leave people in the lurch, but there was absolutely nothing I could do. Pneumonia had me, and I was down. If my grid had been bent toward playing God, I probably would have tried to limp on and perhaps have died on the field of "speaking martyrdom!" (That would have been impressive.)

But I learned a long time ago that no one is indispensable. You do what you can, and after that, you rest in the fact that there really is a God, and you are not him. God is in control. Amazingly, all three conferences went on with great power, and you know what, everyone lived—including me!

If you are to have a straight grid, you must recognize your limitations—accept that you don't have the power to change minds or heal wounds. Only God can do those things. While you can introduce people to the life God offers, only he can give it to them. You can speak the truth in love, but only God can convince people of the truth. You can pray for healing, but only God can heal.

We can lead people as far as they will follow. We can influence others as far as they will be influenced. We can offer suggestions as far as they are open to suggestion. But after that, we have to leave all with the One who loves them more than we could ever hope to.

This means we stop enabling as a way of controlling others. If your son ends up in jail in the middle of the night, let him stay there. Don't try to do anything to help him until morning. You may have to sit on your hands while calling out to God in intense, prevailing prayer, but so be it. It is far better for you to be calling out to God and allowing him to work in your son's life than for you to try to play God in his life.

If you try to be the savior, you will be left holding the responsibility bag while the person who needs the Savior skips off, having evaded his or her need one more time. If people never feel their needs because you have become their earthly need-meeter, then they will have no reason to look to God for help.

Amy Carmichael, the beloved missionary to India, cared for many young students, but because of a debilitating illness, she couldn't help some who were very special to her. She came to the point where she recognized that "some things are allowed to happen so that the quiet power of the Lord to arrange and rearrange events according to His purpose may be shown."[2]

God is working his plan. When you feel anxious or guilty and want to take control, the best way to stay out of God's chair is to pray and ask yourself, "Do I need to jump in, or do I need to rest in what God is doing?"

YOU MEDDLE IN SITUATIONS OVER WHICH YOU HAVE NO AUTHORITY

People with an exaggerated view of their own power often meddle in situations over which they have no authority.

Mary Beth's friend Luann was married to a very difficult man. This drove Mary Beth up a wall. No matter how much she tried to keep out of the fray between Luann and her husband, Mary Beth felt drawn into the battle. Surely there must be something she could do, so she kept meddling. Luann and her husband eventually turned on Mary Beth and told her to butt out of their lives.

Mary Beth was stunned. She thought she was Luann's best friend. The truth was that she had been, but she had overstepped her bounds by trying to fix her friend's marriage. Mary Beth had no authority in this situation, and although her friend drew her into it, she wasn't the one who could change what needed to be changed. If Mary Beth could have seen the wall going up between her and Luann, she could have guessed she needed to back off, but she didn't, and to this day she and Luann remain estranged.

Everyone with a grid bent toward playing God should embrace this truism: "Where there is no authority, there is no responsibility." If you don't have the power to change, mandate, or eradicate, you have nothing to offer. Now, you may think you should meddle, and you may be convinced that so-and-so would be better off if you did meddle, BUT if you have no authority in that situation, then you have no responsibility. It will only strain the relationship for you to give your unsolicited and perhaps unwanted opinion.

Many years ago, I had a friend who was sweet, kind, and precious in so many ways, but she had the notion that if she brought a problem to someone's attention, the person would not only appreciate it but also would immediately change his or her ways. Well, guess what? I found out that she told someone close to me that she might find a better way of interacting with me. She told this person that she needed to talk to me in a different way, because I was hurt by how she addressed me. She had deduced this from watching our interactions, I suppose, although she had very limited knowledge of the relationship. When I heard that she had taken it upon herself to address this matter, needless to say, I was livid. Who did she think she was, meddling with my relationship? I'll give her the benefit of the doubt that her motives were pure, but so help me, her method left more than enough to be desired. I let her know I didn't appreciate her playing God and suggested that from then on she keep such impulses to help to herself.

If you want to live at peace, avoid trying to sit in God's chair. Until your I-have-to-do-something grid is straightened out, you will continue to twist and turn in pure torment. You need to "be still, and know that I am God" (Psalm 46:10, NIV). All of those things that trouble us are under God's direct care and protection. Nothing that matters to you is just floating out there in space waiting for Fate to fly by and determine the outcome. God has you and all that pertains to you under his supervision. Nothing that happens takes him by surprise.

David, whom we read about in the last chapter, eventually became king of Israel. He was also a musician and poet, and he wrote this poem about God's heart toward us when we are up against a really tough situation:

When I walk into the thick of trouble,
    keep me alive in the angry turmoil.
With one hand
    strike my foes,
With your other hand
    save me.
Finish what you started in me, GOD,
    Your love is eternal—don't quit on me now.
        (Psalm 138:7-8, MSG)

Did you catch that? *Finish what you started in me, God, Your love is eternal—don't quit on me now.* This truth can bring amazing comfort and strength. I saw this recently in the response of a friend when her son died from a drug overdose. He had battled with drugs all through his teenage years, and then he developed a relationship with God and stopped using drugs. He wanted to stay clean because of this new relationship, but from the moment he wanted to be clean, he faced a constant struggle. Then one night he slipped back to his old ways, overdosed, and died. My friend and her husband felt devastated. But they also trusted God with every part of their lives, including this precious son who left too early.

On the day of his funeral, his mother was able to stand before the gathered mourners and encourage their hearts with the same encouragement she had received from the Scriptures. "Finish what you started in me, God." She believed that God would finish what needed to be finished for her, her son, and all those who had been touched by his life. Years before her son's death, she had trusted God with his life. She had relinquished any thought she might have entertained of being able to save, change, or heal her son—or any other loved one in her life. She knew her son was in God's hand and that God was the One responsible for what happened to him.

My friend had thoroughly embraced the truth that there is a God, and you are not him. It freed her from despair and gave her peace and hope.

YOU FEEL DISAPPOINTED WITH GOD

If you feel upset with God because he has failed to live up to your expectations, it's another telltale sign that you are sitting in God's chair. Do you have a grid that says, "If I work hard enough, behave properly, and fulfill my religious duties, God is obligated to take care of me in the manner I have come to expect, and if he fails to do so, then I can't trust him"?

This perspective makes you a slave to works. If you fail to attend church, tithe, read your Bible daily, and pray every morning, then you can expect that God will do nothing for you. Conversely, if you do these things, God is obligated to bless you by meeting every need, with some blessings left over!

Have you ever told yourself, "I can tell it's going to be a really bad day; I didn't pray this morning"? Such a perspective sets a trap; you are performing so that God will do what you want him to do.

The problem is that God doesn't respond to us according to what we do, but according to what he wants to do in our lives. He is God. That settles it. All your religious exercises are for your good, not for his benefit. I have seen him bless in spite of me, but I can't name a single time when I could say that God blessed a situation because of something I did. I cannot control God through my actions. He is God. I am not. Why he does what he does, I cannot imagine.

I love the story in the Scriptures about the men who were followers of Christ. On the surface, the story is about some men who go out fishing, when a storm suddenly comes up and scares the pants off them. But in reality, the story is all about Jesus' calming the storm and calming down his disciples. Jesus, the God-man, said to his followers, "Let's go to the other side of the lake." I am sure the boys had great expectations for how that lake crossing was going to look. They were going with the Master, and they loved a boat ride. Who wouldn't be looking forward to that journey?

We pick up the story at the point where Jesus lay down for a nap. Suddenly, a fierce storm began to blow. As it got worse, the disciples watched with horror and concluded, "We are going to drown." They looked at the storm. They looked at their boat. They looked at the sleeping Savior, and they woke him up.

I can just hear all twelve of them screaming above the waves, "Help! Wake up! Help! This boat is going down. We are going to drown." All they could see was the problem. They forgot that they had the Lord of the universe asleep in their boat and that he had said,

"Let's go to the other side." Too many obstacles had come up, and the disciples couldn't help but focus on what had gone wrong instead of what God had told them about their destination.

Ever been there? Have you ever started walking with a destination in mind that you believed God had given you? Have obstacles, frustrations, and delays made you focus on what was going wrong and what you were afraid would happen rather than on what God has spoken to you? If so, then you no doubt know how the disciples felt when Jesus got up, spoke peace to the storm, then turned to them and asked, "Where is your faith? Guys, what are you thinking? I said, 'Let's go to the other side.' Do you think I would let a storm that I can easily silence with a word interfere with my plan for you?"

Like the disciples, we are easily distracted from looking at God's plan and his promise, and we quickly focus on everything that is wrong. Sitting down and giving up in despair, we tell ourselves, "This looks too hard. This looks too scary. I am afraid." At that moment, we miss the joy of the journey. Many of us decide, "I'll just take over now. I really don't trust God to do what he says." Our grid is so twisted that we can see nothing accurately, and our personal plans become far more important than God's plans. We climb up the legs of God's throne, trying to sit in his seat and take over control of our own stuff. What a mistake. We only forfeit his presence, comfort, and compassion.

God is a king, he has a kingdom, and he wants you to be part of it. When you are part of God's kingdom, you can know everything is under control, and you can be at peace. That is what a straight grid is about—having clear vision and a peaceful heart. That will come only as you learn to live as if God is God, and as you give up your choke hold on his position.

YOU BELIEVE YOU WERE SHORTCHANGED

Those who have an inflated view of themselves sometimes feel that God has treated them unfairly. They may never actually voice this thought, but they have a grid that says, "God is a respecter of persons; he likes that person better than he likes me." Your grid needs straightening if you find yourself asking:

- Why is she better looking than I am? (I decided a long time ago that in any given situation, there would always be someone better looking and someone not as good looking as I am. I just needed to focus on how I could bring light and joy to the situation. It was not about my looks or me!)
- Why did he get the job and not me?
- Why did my Mr. Wonderful never come along?
- Why did my Mr. Wonderful turn out to be Mr. Just-Barely-Tolerable?
- Why doesn't God seem to bless me with material things as he does my sister?
- Why do I keep doing things right while my sister-in-law acts like the devil? Yet everyone treats her like a princess!

Can you hear the whine of the list as it piles up? *Why, God? Why?*

Do you look around and see that others are experiencing more of God's favor while you, the faithful one, seem to have been overlooked, declaring, "It just isn't fair!"? Maybe in your way of calling the shots, it isn't fair, but remember God is God and does what he knows is best.

Two of the sharpest women I have known recently died. Both were in their early forties and were vibrant, alive, capable, competent Christ-followers. They both had kingdom passion and great determination and drive to live life to the max. They pursued life until there was nothing left to pursue. In my estimation, both died far too soon. Both could be here today, influencing their world for God's side. He had trusted warriors in those two, but he allowed them to come Home in the middle of their years.

From a human perspective, my friends' deaths were unfair. God could have healed them, and they would be here today telling an incredible story about him. But he didn't choose to heal them. They died and the world is poorer for it. This is hard to swallow. What I find even harder to understand, though, is why others continue to live, drawing easy breaths in spite of their hateful, mean-spirited, God-resistant ways. These people make me want to ask, "Lord, what about them?"

Here is what God says in response to this question:

I am the LORD, and there is no other;
Besides Me there is no God....
That there is no one besides Me.
I am the LORD, and there is no other,
The One forming light and creating darkness,
Causing well-being and creating calamity;
I am the LORD who does all these....

Woe to the one who quarrels with his Maker—
An earthenware vessel among the vessels of earth!
Will the clay say to the potter, "What are you doing?"
(Isaiah 45:5-7,9, NASB)

Makes you think, doesn't it? Have you ever taken on God and quarreled with him over what he was up to? According to this passage, it makes about as much sense as a lump of clay screaming at the potter about what he is doing. The Potter of our lives has the big picture in mind. He can see far beyond our limited view from the potter's wheel. He has the end in sight. We only have the process in view.

It never is easy to relax, watch, and wait, all the while wondering what God is going to do. He is not predictable, nor does he behave in the ways that we always want him to behave. But he always is faithful, and he always is good.

Seek the LORD while He may be found;
Call upon Him while He is near.
Let the wicked forsake his way
And the unrighteous man his thoughts;
And let him return to the LORD,
And He will have compassion on him,
And to our God,
For He will abundantly pardon.
"For My thoughts are not your thoughts,
Nor are your ways My ways," declares the LORD.
"For as the heavens are higher than the earth,

So are My ways higher than your ways
And My thoughts than your thoughts."
(Isaiah 55:6-9, NASB)

That's God's word on the whole deal. He is different. He is above us. But he is compassionate and always ready to pardon and help you move on.

SEEING GOD AS HE IS

Truly, there is a God, and you are not him. He longs to communicate with you, to direct you, to take you down paths that fulfill his plans for you, plans that are for "welfare and not for calamity" (Jeremiah 29:11, NASB). Your job is to view him accurately and to see yourself for who you are in relationship to him.

Isaiah, a prophet who lived thousands of years ago, had a major grid-straightening experience when he saw the Lord for who he is. My friend, if we ever stop long enough to see God as he is and ourselves as we are, we will never be the same.

Take some time to read Isaiah's words and to go with him to the place of straightened grids:

In the year King Uzziah died, I saw the Lord. He was sitting on
a lofty throne, and the train of his robe filled the Temple.
Hovering around him were mighty seraphim, each with six
wings. With two wings they covered their faces, with two they
covered their feet, and with the remaining two they flew. In a

great chorus they sang, "Holy, holy, holy is the LORD Almighty! The whole earth is filled with his glory!" The glorious singing shook the Temple to its foundations, and the entire sanctuary was filled with smoke.

Then I said, "My destruction is sealed, for I am a sinful man and a member of a sinful race. Yet I have seen the King, the LORD Almighty!"

Then one of the seraphim flew over to the altar, and he picked up a burning coal with a pair of tongs. He touched my lips with it and said, "See, this coal has touched your lips. Now your guilt is removed, and your sins are forgiven."

Then I heard the Lord asking, "Whom should I send as a messenger to my people? Who will go for us?"

And I said, "Lord, I'll go! Send me." (Isaiah 6:1-8)

There is a God, and you are not him. Can he use you? Will you let him? Your willingness to be used is in direct proportion to your understanding of who is in control. The healing that comes with a straightened grid may give you another way to look at some issues in your life. Take the time to do it. Your adventure with God is only beginning!

NINE

ATTITUDE IS EVERYTHING

When life hands you a lemon, say, "O, yeah, I like lemons. What else you got?"

—HENRY ROLLINS

I learned a long time ago that attitude truly is everything. If you view people as controllers of your happiness, then guess what? You will allow them to have control of your joy. If you think that people are out to scam you, then you will be wary and distrustful in your relationships. If you see yourself as limited and uninteresting, no doubt about it, you will fulfill that description. If you think you are unattractive, then no matter what you do to compensate, you will feel as if you just don't measure up.

Attitude is everything. A bad attitude will inevitably yield poor results while a good attitude will give you the emotional upper hand every time. As I have said over and over: Life happens. We don't determine what will happen, but we surely can say how we will respond to what happens.

I had to apply this truth recently in one of those annoying-but-not-the-end-of-the-world situations. I booked a ticket to Colorado that had a stopover in Dallas. Then I decided to spend the night with a friend, so I changed my ticket to return a day later. Well, little did I know that changing my ticket would put me at the top of the list as a major security risk!

As soon as I arrived at the airport in Chattanooga for the first leg of the trip, the searches began. I was stopped, frisked, and searched at all three airports at every point—five times in all. Let me tell you, this was an attitude-challenging experience, particularly when I was escorted with my large checked luggage to a little cubicle where a woman inspector said, "Everything has to come out of that suitcase!"

I choked. "Everything?"

"Yes ma'am, everything."

I watched as she started with my fingernail polish and worked her way through underwear, cosmetics, clothes (hanging and folded), shoes, pajamas, and some books I had acquired on the way.

As she pulled out my stuff, piece by piece, she chatted away like a fishwife doing her laundry with a friend. With her back to me and her hands touching everything I owned, she told me about having an empty nest and that she was a country music fan. She told me, "I plan to make it to the Grand Ole Opry in Nashville, someday! I want to hear all those stars—you know, Travis Tritt, Loretta Lynn"—and then she rattled off a list of newcomers I had never heard of. She is a fan. And she was a security guard at a busy airport who likely had to deal with angry, frustrated people all day long—yet here she was, talking to me like I was a friend.

I knew I had a choice. Either I could be cranky about having my luggage searched *again,* or I could choose to be pleasant and to enjoy our conversation. I chose to be pleasant, and we chatted away.

When she finally packed everything back in my bag, piece by piece, trying to get it back like I had it, she closed it up and turned to me with a big smile. As she handed me my luggage, she said, "God bless you," and I said, "God bless you," and we hugged like long-lost cousins.

As I walked out on the concourse, I had to smile. Who would

have thought that I would be hugging the security person who had just riffled through all of my personal belongings? We both had chosen to make the best of our situations. We both had made the decision to live above what had been imposed on us.

Attitude is everything. But a good attitude isn't automatic, particularly if you have a grid that is bent toward the negative.

CHOOSING A POSITIVE ATTITUDE

One of my favorite stories is about a guy who was a crew chief for military airplanes during World War II. He was seen one day trying to get one of those huge Flying Fortresses out of the mud, where it was securely lodged. It was raining and miserable. The crew chief was whistling and working away. When asked, "Why are you whistling with a mess like this?" the crew chief replied, "When the facts won't budge, you have to bend your attitude to fit them."[1]

Here's the deal. We just have to choose whether we are going to let the facts bend us or whether we are going to bend our attitudes to transcend the facts.

Now I am not a proponent of the kind of positive thinking that says you are only supposed to believe what you want to be true versus what is true. I don't think that has to do with attitude. That is denial. Don't deny what is true, but remember that attitude is everything. You can determine what your attitude will be toward that truth.

Scripture tells of a man who didn't deny that life was tough but instead chose to adopt a positive attitude—Paul, the apostle. When we first read about him, Paul was persecuting Christians, but he was stopped in his tracks when Christ confronted him on the road to Damascus. Paul had a dramatic turnaround and became a follower of "The Way," which was what many people called the religion of the early church. Paul's former associates, who were the religious leaders of the day, weren't happy about his change of heart. Suddenly, Paul became the target for all kinds of persecutions. He was beaten, run out of town, slandered, and misunderstood. Those are the facts. Paul didn't deny them by saying, "Oh, I have been treated so wonderfully, and I am outrageously blessed," but rather he said,

> Who will separate us from the love of Christ? Will tribulation, or distress, or persecution, or famine, or nakedness, or peril, or sword? Just as it is written, *"For your sake we are being put to death all day long; we were considered as sheep to be slaughtered."* But in all these things we overwhelmingly conquer through Him who loved us. For I am convinced that neither death, nor life, nor angels, nor principalities, nor things present, nor things to come, nor powers, nor height, nor depth, nor any other created thing, will be able to separate us from the love of God, which is in Christ Jesus our Lord. (Romans 8:35-39, NASB, emphasis added)

That's a winning attitude from a guy who ultimately ended up in a Roman prison, chained to a guard and kept from the freedom he loved. Through it all, his attitude was positive.

DO YOU NEED AN ATTITUDE ADJUSTMENT?

If your grid has a bent toward the negative, you will always prepare yourself for the worst. You think:

- If someone is going to mess up, it will be me.
- If there's a disaster looking for a place to happen, it will find me.
- I'm already preparing myself for the disappointment. I probably won't get the job.

This was true of two friends of mine whose grids were skewed toward the negative. One had such a pessimistic view that she would not tell anyone what athletic team she was rooting for because she believed if she was for a team, they were doomed to lose. The other had the motto, "Hope for the best, but expect the worst."

You don't have to live this way. Ironically, it's just as easy to put on a good attitude as it is a bad one, but sometimes we don't even stop to consider that we have a choice—but we do.

When you see people go through tough times with a good attitude, do you wonder if you could do the same? Do you wonder how you can get your attitude adjusted? You can, if you are willing to straighten your grid.

I believe there are certain graces you can practice and extend to others that will straighten your grid when it comes to your attitude. You'll be amazed at how going ahead and choosing to do these acts can straighten your grid and lift your spirits. Your thoughts will be softer, calmer, and more loving.

What are these acts?

Forgive...even if it seems irrational.

Give...even when it's undeserved.

Praise...even when you are disappointed.

Forgive...Even If It Seems Irrational

If you stay caught up in the facts of someone's transgression toward you, your attitude toward him or her will remain hard and unyielding. Left unchecked, unforgiveness will make you bitter. Forgiveness is the only act that can relieve you from that hardness and set you free from the offense. If you forgive, you will be better off.

This can be hard to swallow, especially in the face of some atrocious, careless, or harmful behavior. But forgiveness literally detaches you from the offense and the offender and sets you free to get on with your life. I have found that when I forgive, I become neutral toward the one who has offended me. It is as if the act of forgiveness neutralizes the offense and straightens my grid. I am able to see things as they are, but I am not tangled up in some web of trying to make it all right. I don't stay attached to the offense. Forgiveness eventually enables me to see the person as he or she really is because I'm not focused on the offense.

Forgiveness is a breath of fresh air. It softens your heart and helps you keep on going toward healthier living.

In her best-selling book *Traveling Mercies: Some Thoughts on Faith*, Anne Lamott tells about one of those need-to-forgive-but-don't-want-to-forgive situations. When her son, Sam, was in first grade, there was a particularly aggravating woman, another parent, who offended the stew out of Anne. She was one of those perfect, always in control, caustic individuals you love to hate. Anne had come to faith and knew she needed to forgive this woman's obnoxious behavior and sarcastic remarks.

She said that everywhere she turned—from fortune cookies to skywriting—she ran into reminders that she needed to forgive this woman. She writes:

> Then in a few days, I was picking Sam up at the house of another friend and noticed a yellowed clipping taped to the refrigerator with FORGIVENESS written at the top—as though God had decided to abandon all efforts at subtlety and just plain nudge. The clipping said that God was *for giving* and that we are here for giving, too, and that to withhold love or blessings is to be completely delusional.[2]

Anne copied down the thought, took it home, and before long she found herself in this woman's home because Sam had been invited there to play. Anne had a grid-straightening moment when she realized her attitude toward the other woman was as bad or worse. She realized that she needed to be forgiven as much as or more than this other woman. So she began acting out the choice she was making. She writes, "I felt so happy there in her living room that I got drunk on her tea.… I started speaking sweetly to everyone—to the mother, to the boys."[3] When Anne practiced forgiveness, she became free. Her grid was straight and life looked different because of it.

Even as I write this, I can think of some people who are going to be faced with the choice to forgive or not to forgive:

- A young man was thrown from his car and critically injured because of the behavior of a drunk driver. It was the drunk driver's third DUI. To see him on the news was repugnant. In his state of alcoholic confusion, he stumbled about while the police were trying to cuff him. A twenty-one-year-old was clinging to life because this guy was drunk.

- A young couple lost their baby daughter when her male baby-sitter shook her violently.

- A dump truck crossed the median hitting a car with four people in it head-on. The truck driver was driving on a suspended license. He lived. They all died instantly.

In each of these situations, forgiveness seems irrational. But the truth is, forgiveness is never offered to those who deserve it. When you offer forgiveness, you are offering grace to another person. That's the way forgiveness works. It's offered to those who don't deserve it. It is totally unmerited, and the choice to offer it is in your hands, even as you realize that the other person may not change or even care whether you forgive him or her. But if you choose forgiveness, you have chosen to take control of your emotions.

Given the alternative of holding on to the pain and the hurt and the loss, wouldn't you want to make the choice to forgive? Until you can forgive, you are tied to the situation, and your whole life will be affected by it. Refusing to forgive is saying, "I intend to hold on to the feelings, the pain, the hurt, the struggles. However all of that affects the way I view life, so be it."

So even if it seems irrational, forgive. You can't forgive and keep a cold heart. Somehow, the act itself blows away the cobwebs of misery, and your heart becomes pliable in God's hands.

One of my dear friends recently did the work to forgive her father, and forgiveness has set her free to be who she is and to relate to her dad in a new and more mature way. Her dad was the head of a big family. He had a loving wife and a prosperous career, but his feelings for his secretary took him down a road of ruin that would eventually leave his whole family torn apart. He left his family and married his secretary. His adult children could not believe that this was their father who had always been so upright and respected.

Eventually their father told them he was sorry for his actions, but by then the damage had been done. They were hurt and unable to trust him. What would they do with their pain?

My friend chose, deliberately and openly, to forgive her daddy and his new wife. Because she has, she can visit with her aging dad and spend time with his wife and him without feelings of hardness and bitterness. She sent away the offense, disconnected herself from the power of the situation, and consequently, she is free.

Her act of forgiveness doesn't change what her father did nor does it take away the pain that his actions caused, but it did help adjust her attitude so that she isn't angry and resentful toward him. Forgiveness helps make today a better day because yesterday is not overshadowing it.

Forgiveness works. You can't forgive and, at the same time, hang on to your negative attitude about a person. Forgiveness brings healing and hope—and hope always translates into a positive attitude.

Give…Even When It's Undeserved

Giving is another attitude adjuster. You just can't give to others and hold on to a negative attitude at the same time. I can't explain why giving to others clears your grid and softens your heart, but I know it does. When we give to others—with no strings attached—God is pleased. We know we've done something right and good—and that changes our attitudes!

I recently went to lunch with my daughters-in-law and their children (my sweet grandchildren). As we sat down, our waiter came up to the table and threw the coasters down one by one. He acted like a man who had had a bad day, and we were catching him at the tail end of it. Everything seemed like one big effort to him. He carelessly put the silverware down, barely acknowledged our presence, and made it evident through his indifference that he'd rather not be serving us.

The girls and I had a choice. We could act as he was acting by sighing, rolling our eyes, and letting him know in many not-so-subtle ways that he had our attention and we were going to join him in his behavior, or we could choose to bless him in spite of himself. We chose the latter. We decided that we would try to make his world a little better. We cleaned up all the crumbs the children left (which weren't many), then left him a great tip.

It was definitely a choice to leave him a good tip, as there was nothing about him that made me want to bless him. He wasn't cute or personable or winsome. He wasn't simply unhelpful—he was downright rude. (Frankly, I didn't like him.) But once I decided to bless him, my attitude toward him changed. I saw that he was tired, bored, and unhappy. I felt compassion for him instead of anger and irritation. Giving made the difference.

Of course, it doesn't work to give to others if we do it simply to get something back—even if that something is a better attitude. When we give, we must give from our heart, and happily. God loves a cheerful giver. I love this scripture that reminds us of that attitude:

You must each make up your own mind as to how much you should give. Don't give reluctantly or in response to pressure. For God loves the person who gives cheerfully. (2 Corinthians 9:7)

I am a giver because God has given many good things to me. Whether anyone deserves it is not the issue. Giving helps clear my grid, which can be very tangled with self-serving. If I am looking to give to others, I can't be all tangled up with myself. When I give, I am living out one of the reasons I am on the planet.

Try it. You will love it. Here are some ideas to get you started:
- Find the maid at the hotel, and give her twenty dollars for no special reason.
- Leave a small gift on a difficult coworker's desk.
- Give a rose to a friend who has been distracted with her own life.
- Send a charitable donation in honor of a teacher you didn't particularly like when you were in high school.
- Keep some bills of small denomination in your purse whenever you travel. Service people are blessed when you tip them beyond their expectation.

- Give a gift "just because" to an unsuspecting recipient.
- Send a card with money in it for a meal to a young couple who has just gotten married.

I will never forget one of the times I did something like this. Sometimes when I was out driving, I would see a young woman walking along the side of the road in her restaurant uniform. I would pick her up a couple of times and give her a ride to her job. She always thanked me profusely. One day when I was out driving along that same road, I remembered I had some extra money in my wallet, so I took it out and put it in my right pocket, just in case I saw her that day. Sure enough, there she was walking in the hot sun on her way to work, so I stopped and picked her up. We talked about her little boy who stayed home by himself. We talked about her job, and soon we were at her restaurant. As she opened the door to get out, I slipped the money into her hand and told her that God loves her and that this was a gift for her. She was thrilled and so was I.

I didn't give in order get anything from this woman. In fact, I never saw her again. I gave just for the pure joy of giving.

Praise...Even When You Are Disappointed

When the stress piles up and you are disappointed with how things are going, you have a choice. You can praise or you can pout. That's about what it amounts to. You can make the conscious decision to be grateful to this God who is in control, or you can pout because things haven't gone your way.

There are plenty of situations that can bring your spirits down. When things aren't going well, we can blame God for what is wrong and retreat to our personal arena of pouting and self-pity, or we can make a choice to praise him for who he is. When we praise God in the midst of negative circumstances, we are choosing to trust that he is loving and good. Such praise is sweet to him because it honors him for who he is—God—and not because he has given us what we want in life. Such praise is a sweet sacrifice to God.

In praise, we recognize who God is—and that changes our perspective unlike anything else, for it reminds us of who we are as well. You can't praise God and have a bad attitude or feel sorry for yourself.

I was reminded of this several months ago when I met a man on a hydrofoil crossing the sea between Hong Kong and mainland China. I was with a small group of believers who were going to the mainland to encourage other believers. The man sitting next to me was a pastor who had been imprisoned for his faith for fifteen years. Now he was free and was going back and forth to China to keep encouraging those who believed.

We traveled together for more than an hour, so he asked me if I would like to hear his story. Of course I said yes. He told me: "I was imprisoned for preaching the gospel. I had a guard posted right by me twenty-four hours a day. I could go nowhere in that camp without a guard but one place, and that was the night soil pit. They hated the stench of that place and the flies that swarmed around it eternally. So I asked to be assigned to work at the night soil pit. If I could, then I knew I would have some time alone to be with my Lord."

He continued, "I got the assignment, and every morning I would get up before dawn and make my way to the pit. I would always sing that old hymn, 'I Come to the Garden Alone.' That was my praise time. That was my time to worship. That is what allowed me to survive the fifteen years of beatings and ill treatment. I could offer praise."

This man's words blew me away. He really knew what it meant to offer the sacrifice of praise. We can't praise God and have an attitude that says, "Woe is me" or "Things are only going to get worse from here." When we praise God for the good and the bad, we are announcing to all who know us that there is a God and that we truly believe he is good.

AN ATTITUDE OF GLADNESS

Martin and Gracia Burnham's attitude was notably good and gracious while they were in captivity in the Philippines. Serving as missionaries there, the Burnhams had gone to a beach resort to celebrate their eighteenth wedding anniversary. A Muslim extremist group, Abu Sayyaf, burst into the resort without warning and took them and others captive for over a year.

During that time, they were moved from place to place, from one dirty little encampment to another. At night Martin was chained to a tree so he could not escape, yet he would thank the guards and often talked with them about Jesus. He was forced to carry heavy bags of rice and would often slip in the rain, yet he never complained.

One day toward the end of their captivity, Martin and Gracia were very tired and sat down to rest in their hammock. Martin told Gracia, "It's been a very hard year, but it's been a very good year," and they began to thank the Lord for everything they could think of. They thanked the Lord for their hammock and their boots and the loan of a rebel radio so they could hear the Voice of America. This was the last thing they did together before Martin's death. After thanking God for his faithfulness, they lay down for a nap, only to be awakened by a firefight between rebels and the Philippine Rangers who had come to rescue the Burnhams.

As a result of the firefight, Martin was killed and Gracia was wounded.

At Martin's memorial service, Gracia told how during their captivity God had brought Psalm 100:2 to her husband's mind: "Serve the LORD with gladness: come before his presence with singing" (KJV). He said, "We might not leave the jungle alive, but at least we will leave this world serving the Lord with gladness. We can serve him right here where we are with gladness."[4]

Attitude is everything. It determines your demeanor. It affects what you say or don't say. It is reflected in your eyes. It shows up in your choices to be kind or patient when you are a hairsbreadth away from snapping someone's head off. When mixed with life's circumstances, a good attitude brings light to darkness, hope to despair, joy to gloom, and a sense of peace when the grumps have taken over the conversation.

Your attitude will determine the course of your life. If you can learn to have a positive attitude, then you will have mastered an art that will get you places that you want to go. A positive attitude straightens your grid and keeps it straight as long as you maintain the attitude. So here's to your strong, positive attitude. It is yours for the choosing. It is yours to enjoy.

TEN

THE LAST CHAPTER HAS NOT YET BEEN WRITTEN

Twenty years from now you will be more disappointed by the things you didn't do than by the ones you did do. So, throw off the bowlines. Sail away from the safe harbor. Catch the trade winds in your sails. Explore. Dream. Discover.

—MARK TWAIN

Joe Parks lived every day to the fullest. A musician and a composer, he understood that each day brought with it the potential for him to write a new song—and he did. Joe made music, not just with instruments and notes, but with his life. Although he died suddenly at the age of sixty-three, he did not waste a moment.

Joe knew how to encourage people. As a teacher, he helped many young musicians believe in themselves. He gave his sons a vision for what they could be. He wrote music for large as well as small church choirs. Although there wasn't much fame or fortune in that kind of composing, Joe wanted every church to enjoy the same quality music and composing. He brought a smile to every occasion, no matter what it was.

In the year before he died, Joe and his wife, Wilda, frequently took walks together and sat on a favorite rock to watch the sunset. They lived on a gorgeous mountain in Tennessee, so the views were spectacular. Joe often wanted to linger after the sun had set. He would tell Wilda, "I just want to squeeze everything I can out of this day." So until the last ray was gone, he and the woman he loved sat absorbing the gift they had been given—life.

Joe died prematurely by some people's standards, but I doubt that he would agree. While he was alive, he *lived*. He savored each moment for what it was. He lived as if the last chapter had not yet been written—right up to the last period of the last chapter in his life.

I believe that God wants each of us to live this way, to live with joy and anticipation. God is the marvelous Author of our biography. He has plans for us, plans to give us a future and a hope. He has plans to prosper us, not to harm us (see Jeremiah 29:11). Our God has plans, and he wants us to join him in the great adventure of living life—right up to the last minute—because the last chapter hasn't been written yet.

Only God knows when our last chapter will be written, and none of us will live beyond the boundary set for us. Knowing that God has already determined the end can free you to get on with the business of living instead of worrying about when you'll die (see Job 14:5; Psalm 31:15).

Here's the deal. You are going to die. You don't know when, but God does. He is writing your biography with plans, a future, and hopes. What you may perceive as a setback or a roadblock is all part of the plan. You may have made some poor choices—even destructive choices—but God can use them to get you where he wants you to go. He is directing your journey, and in his plan, even death is not the final chapter. In his plan, death is merely the transition between part 1 and part 2.

So live your life to the max. Live wisely and trust God.

I love this waggish quote from Eileen Guder found in her book *God, But I'm Bored:*

> You can live on bland food so as to avoid an ulcer, drink no tea or coffee or other stimulants in the name of health, go to bed early and stay away from night life, avoid all controversial sub-

jects so as never to give offense, mind your own business and
not get involved in other people's problems, spend money only
on necessities and save all you can. You can still break your neck
in the bathtub, and it will serve you right.[1]

Life is to be lived and not tippytoed around! Stuff happens, and
no matter what you do, if it's going to happen, it happens. Sometimes
it's the very thing you have worked hard to avoid that gets you, like
what happened to a woman I knew who was a health food fanatic.
She never ate anything but unprocessed food. She took vitamins by
the handful and died of stomach cancer in her fifties. What good did
her strict regimens do her?

Don't let life pass you by because you are too cautious to really
live. If God hasn't written the last chapter, then your life on earth isn't
over yet—so don't act as if it is, regardless of your circumstances, no
matter what you've done.

IF YOUR LIFE AIN'T OVER, DON'T ACT LIKE IT IS

Miss Arvine Bell was my camp director over forty years ago. I loved
her for her leadership qualities and for being uniquely herself. She was
short yet large and had a formidable presence. She could corral 180
girls just by standing in front of us and raising her very ample hand
for attention. Trust me, she had it! We would fall silent, waiting for
what she had to say. We didn't wiggle. She never had to say anything
or apply any discipline. We just knew it was time to be quiet, and we
were quiet. Miss Bell had spoken. About the time we were all confident

the wrath of God was going to fall on us, she would smile her Jack Nicholson smile and say, "Schweeties, always remember who you are, where you are from, and what you represent." No one wanted to be any less than Miss Bell expected—and she expected a lot!

Miss Bell came to Crestridge from a college where she had been a coach. That was in 1959. When she reached her late sixties, Miss Bell retired from camp life. A few years later I lost track of her. Then one summer I returned to camp for a reunion and heard the news that Miss Bell had just died. But I knew she hadn't "just died." I knew that there had to be more to the story. That was not her way.

Miss Bell wanted her ashes to be scattered at camp (that was so Miss Bell). Those of us who had been campers when she was in her prime gathered in the woods and quoted from Psalm 121: "I will lift up mine eyes unto the hills from whence cometh my help" (verse 1, KJV). We sang the camp song and scattered her ashes.

A friend who was close to Miss Bell in her latter years sent a letter with her ashes and told about her last days. She had had emergency heart bypass surgery that went awry, and she died from the complications. It was obvious she didn't know that she was living her last chapter. Before she went into the hospital, she had been writing a Bible study for the young women in her hometown. The surgery wasn't on her agenda, but she made great effort to be sure everyone she came in contact with was comforted and was met with kind words of encouragement and an introduction to a relationship with God. She only had a few days in the hospital before she went into surgery. As far as she knew, she was just making new friends on the journey. She didn't know God was about to pen The End to her earthly story. She lived the last page of her last chapter just as she had lived all the others, even when she knew she was seriously ill. She didn't go into surgery planning to wake up in heaven. She planned to wake up in Arkansas, so she didn't act like someone about to die.

I hope you don't either.

You might have a hard time believing that God has other chapters for you to live, particularly if you have a chronic or terminal illness. But if you are breathing, God's still writing, and you still have some living to do. Don't allow the limitations of compromised health to take all of the joy of living right out of you. Look around you—and live with all the gusto you can.

GOD CAN REDEEM YOUR MESSES

No matter what you've done, no matter what you've gotten yourself into, God can redeem your messes. If you are willing to let him get into your stuff and deal with it, he will fill you with hope and joy. As long as you have breath, God has purpose for your life, and your job is to be about living it.

Iris Blue will tell you. She is living proof that bad choices don't always call for last chapters. Her teenage years had been tough. She felt self-conscious about her height—she was six feet three inches tall—and was very insecure. In her anxious desire to be accepted, Iris got involved with the wrong crowd and found herself in prison for seven years for being an accessory to armed robbery. She spent three of those years in solitary confinement because she had fought with the other inmates. They would pick on her because she was big, so she would take them on.

When Iris had served her time and got out of prison, she went right back to her old way of life, doing drugs and hanging out in strip bars. She slept with any man who would have her, and she had several abortions. One night a young evangelist came into the bar and tried to tell her about a relationship with God through Jesus Christ. Iris wanted nothing to do with religion or Jesus, so she tried to avoid him—and if she couldn't do that, she would humiliate him. But he kept coming back and telling her the same thing. Then one night he came to tell her that he couldn't come back to the bar anymore. The atmosphere was getting to him. Then he told her, "You are nothing but a tramp."

His words stung Iris's heart, and she told him, "You are probably right, but honestly, all I ever wanted to be was a lady."

Now he was the one who was stung. All of his efforts had failed, and this was all she wanted? "If that is all, why didn't you say so? Jesus can make you a lady."

That night in a strip club, with needle marks up and down her arm and stringy, long green hair hanging down her back, Iris Blue knelt down as a tramp and got up as a lady. Ever since that day, Iris has been telling people about Jesus. She has spoken in churches, prisons, and youth meetings all around the world. Twenty years ago you would have thought that Iris would never change, would never live a rich, full life. But a few chapters later, she embarked on a grand and glorious adventure.

Iris's story is still being written. And if you are reading this book, so is yours—even if people tell you otherwise. So don't listen to these naysayers.

John Mark can tell you that they don't know what they are talking about. When his path crossed with that great, strong-willed apostle Paul, John Mark became a disciple. He traveled with Paul to work with him in the ministry, but at one difficult spot in their travels, John Mark bailed out. The Scriptures say, "Now Paul and his companions put out to sea from Paphos and came to Perga in Pamphylia; but John [Mark] left them and returned to Jerusalem" (Acts 13:13, NASB). Bad move, John Mark. Paul is so over you!

Later on, Paul's good friend in the ministry, Barnabas, wanted John Mark to join him and Paul on a missionary journey. This did not sit well with Paul, who had decided that John Mark was more of a liability than an asset. He had deserted them in Pamphylia, and as far as Paul was concerned, that disqualified John Mark from being useful. In Paul's eyes, John Mark was a quitter. But Barnabas didn't see things that way, and he talked with Paul about it, but they absolutely could not agree. So Paul went one way and Barnabas another (see Acts 15:37-39).

Those must have been tough days for John Mark. After all, it's not every day you have a powerful apostle so displeased with your behavior that he tells you your days of ministry are over. How could he live that down?

But God had some more chapters to write in John Mark's story.

When the apostle Paul was at the end of his life, he wrote a letter to Timothy. Paul was in prison in Rome and needed Timothy to come to him. He said, "Only Luke is with me. Pick up [John] Mark and bring him with you, for he is useful to me for service" (2 Timothy 4:11, NASB).

Just because others tell you that you have done something that's ruined your life, that doesn't make it true. The last chapter has not been written yet. John Mark's hadn't been—and neither has yours.

HOLDING ON TO HOPE FOR THOSE YOU LOVE

When I speak on this topic at conferences, I find that it's easier for people to believe this truth for themselves than to believe it for loved ones they are concerned about. If this is your situation, ask God to help you hold on to the truth that the last chapter has not yet been written for those you love either.

Want to know how I can be so sure?

In the Scriptures there is a great story of a well-loved son who decided that he wanted to go away and live it up. He asked for his inheritance, and his father gave it to him. It wasn't long until the son packed up all his gear and took a trip into a distant land. He couldn't resist the temptations, so it wasn't long until he spent all of his inheritance. The party boy was totally without funds. Unfortunately, the economy went belly up, and this well-loved bad boy went belly up with it. He did have enough ingenuity to ask a farmer if he could have a job feeding his pigs. He was hired on, and it wasn't long before the pigs' food began to look good to him. No one had pity on him, because they all had their own issues. He was left without food, home, or friends. Times were tough, tougher than he had ever thought they would be. Life back home had been good, and he wanted to go back, whether they wanted him or not. He just wanted to go home.

> When he finally came to his senses, he said to himself, "At home even the hired men have food enough to spare, and here I am, dying of hunger! I will go home to my father and say, 'Father, I have sinned against both heaven and you, and I am no longer worthy of being called your son. Please take me on as a hired man.'" (Luke 15:17-19)

So he went home to his father. He was exhausted and wasn't sure what awaited him, but anything would be better than what he had been through in the far land. When he got near the home place, his father saw him in the distance and came running. His dad grabbed him in the biggest bear hug he had ever had and told him how much he had missed him and how much he loved him. What a welcome home!

The son said, "I have really messed up. I've gone against everything you ever taught me about love and God and living right. I don't deserve to have you speak to me or even call me your son but I want you to know I am sorry."

> But his father said to the servants, "Quick! Bring the finest robe in the house and put it on him. Get a ring for his finger, and sandals for his feet. And kill the calf we have been fattening in the pen. We must celebrate with a feast, for this son of mine was dead and has now returned to life. He was lost, but now he is found." So the party began. (Luke 15:22-24)

The last chapter was not written the day that boy went into a far country, and the last chapter is not written when your son or daughter or husband or friend or mother or father goes into a far country. The last chapter is written when God writes it—and not until!

Here's the deal:

As long as there is life, there is hope. You cannot ever second-guess what God is going to do or what influences will be brought to bear on you or anyone else. Of course, I believe the Spirit behind those influences is God. He is the One who draws people to life and wholeness.

Prayer works long after we have left the scene. That's the great part about prayer. You don't have to be present to collect the reward. You can already be living part 2 of your story after you have left this earth, and your prayers will keep on being effective. You pray and God works, but he is not confined to your calendar or your lifetime. How neat is that?

Jesus prayed for you and me when he was praying for his followers. He included us when he said, "My prayer is not for them alone. I pray also for those who will believe in me through their message" (John 17:20, NIV).

I know a family that was decimated by the drunken lifestyle of an alcoholic father. He finally left, and the mother and grandmother raised the children. The grandmother prayed. Her heart was committed to God, and she made prayer a habit of her life. All three of the children survived the trauma of their childhood and are living lives of wholeness and productivity. They could have been in a trash heap somewhere, but the last chapter wasn't written when their father left.

The last chapter still has not been written. We won't know their completed story until it comes to an end, but surely prayer has had an impact on them.

God cares more about your loved one than you do. And since he does, you can count on him to do what is best for that person. More often than not, the best thing you can do is stay out of the way. Well-intentioned advice, admonitions, and rebukes muddy the picture. God deals with a recalcitrant individual in his own unique way. Sometimes it may seem harsh or perhaps overly easy, but one thing's for sure: Once the task is put in God's hands, he will see it through to completion. The last chapter may not come out the way you want it to, but if the one you love truly has been placed in God's hands, you have placed that loved one in the safest place he or she can be. You will have done more for that person than anything else you could do.

YOU CAN'T LOSE

God has made it clear that he is willing to work in our lives to make the things that may be hard, difficult, or even completely unmanageable turn out for our good. That's his promise to those who have a relationship with him. *The Message* puts it this way:

> We can be so sure that every detail in our lives of love for God
> is worked into something good.
>
> God knew what he was doing from the very beginning. He
> decided from the outset to shape the lives of those who love
> him along the same lines as the life of his Son....

So, what do you think? With God on our side like this,
how can we lose? (Romans 8:28-29,31)

You can't lose when you are connected to God. Even when things are stressful, God still brings the stars out every night, the birds still go about their daily chores, sunsets are still gorgeous, and morning follows night with unbelievable regularity. These things you can know and enjoy—and there are many, many more.

So look around and really see all the good things that are in your life. Live and live fully.

CONCLUSION

My friend, if your grid brings you emotional excesses and pain, don't wait to do something about it. The time to do the work required for grid straightening is NOW, so that when the difficult, the hard, and the seemingly impossible events of life show up, your grid will be straighter and your perspective clearer, and you'll be able to look at what happens in a different, healthier way.

The clarity of truth is a wonderful thing. When your grid is straight, you will no longer wonder, *Am I thinking the right thing here?* You won't have to ask, "Did I say the right thing?" You won't always be looking for little hidden pockets of half-truth that can trip you up. You will live through hard, hard things and come out on the other side as one who "overwhelmingly conquer[s] through Him who loved us" (Romans 8:37, NASB). The "Him" is God, and he is into making conquerors out of those who feel defeated!

Most Christians understand that we have to guard our minds from impure thoughts, the Enemy's deception, and the influence of corrupt companions, but few of us have grabbed hold of the reality that we can influence the way we see life, and if our perspective is clouded or skewed, with God's help we can clear away the fog and see what really is.

The apostle Paul called the readers of his letter to the Philippians to follow sound grid-straightening practices—practices he himself obviously employed. He said, "I got it, and I want you to get it too, because then the God of peace will be with you." Read his words in chapter 4:

> Don't worry about anything; instead, pray about everything. Tell God what you need, and thank him for all he has done. If you do this, you will experience God's peace, which is far more wonderful than the human mind can understand. His peace will guard your hearts and minds as you live in Christ Jesus.
>
> And now, dear brothers and sisters, let me say one more thing as I close this letter. Fix your thoughts on what is true and honorable and right. Think about things that are pure and lovely and admirable. Think about things that are excellent and worthy of praise. Keep putting into practice all you learned from me and heard from me and saw me doing, and the God of peace will be with you. (verses 6-9)

When your grid is straightened with the truth, and you are living life with a clear perspective, you'll begin telling yourself and your friends to "look at it this way." You will know that:

- This is one event in a lifetime of events.
- What might have been does not exist.
- "They said" doesn't make it true.
- If something doesn't work, change it.
- Fretting only destroys you.
- Don't tell everything you know.
- Feeling guilty doesn't mean you are.
- There is a God, and you are not him.

- Attitude is everything.
- The last chapter has not yet been written.

There's no magic in these words, but the truth indeed does set us free (see John 8:32). I assure you that if you will practice these maxims—and make them part of your thought choices no matter what is going on—you will be a changed person. You'll enjoy a healthy, peaceful mind, emotional well-being, and spiritual confidence. In turn, you will experience ever-improving relationships.

Sounds like a tall promise, doesn't it? I understand, but trust me. If your life isn't working and you find yourself ruled by emotions, then you will never regret embracing these solid truths about how life works.

NOTES

Introduction

1. Bill O'Hanlon, *Do One Thing Different* (New York: HarperCollins, 1999), 110-1.

Chapter 4

1. O'Hanlon, *Do One Thing Different,* 6-7.
2. O'Hanlon, *Do One Thing Different,* 6-7.

Chapter 5

1. Fawn Germer, *Hard Won Wisdom* (New York: Perigee Books, 2001), 173.

Chapter 8

1. William Backus, *Telling Each Other the Truth* (Minneapolis: Bethany, 1991), 57.
2. Amy Carmichael, *Candles in the Dark* (Fort Washington, Pa.: Christian Literature Crusade, 1982), 50.

Chapter 9

1. Robert Andrews, *The Columbia Dictionary of Quotations* (New York: Columbia University, 1993).
2. Anne Lamott, *Traveling Mercies: Some Thoughts On Faith* (New York: Random House, 1999), 136-7.

3. Lamott, *Traveling Mercies,* 136-7.

4. E-mail correspondence regarding Martin Burnham's memorial service.

Chapter 10

1. Eileen Guder, *God, But I'm Bored* (New York: Doubleday, 1971), quoted in Charles R. Swindoll, *The Tale of the Tardy Oxcart and 1,501 Other Stories* (Nashville: Word, 1998), 344.

ABOUT THE AUTHOR

JAN SILVIOUS is an author and speaker with a passion for offering hope and encouragement to those who are stuck in their life circumstances. She speaks at conferences and seminars both nationally and internationally.

Jan was on staff at Precept Ministries for more than a decade and co-hosted a live call-in radio program with Kay Arthur for five years. She leads women's seminars for Moody Bible Institute's conference ministry and is also a regular speaker for Women of Faith.

Jan has been married to her husband, Charlie, for more than forty years. They have three grown sons and several grandchildren. They make their home in Chattanooga, Tennessee.